THE CHICKEN-WARRIOR AND
THE DIVORCE ATTORNEY

THE CHICKEN-WARRIOR AND THE DIVORCE ATTORNEY

PATHWAY TO SELF-EMPOWERMENT AND HEALING

Michael Buttacavoli

CONTENTS

1.	The Encounter	1
2.	Adagio	4
3.	Thirty Days after Encounter	5
4.	Doings	8
5.	The Frost	10
6.	Eruption	12
7.	The Starting Point	16
8.	Before the Storm	19
9.	The State Bar of Hades	21
10.	Rollo La Rue	25
11.	Crucial Tactic	30
12.	The Most Important Question You Can Ask	32
13.	How to Choose an Attorney	34
14.	A Critical Skill	36
15.	Collaborative Law Model	38
16.	Goals	40
17.	Detailed Itemized Bill	42
18.	Cost of Divorce	43

19.	Cost Reduction Strategy	48
20.	Mediation	51
21.	Stipulation	56
22.	Productivity of Motions	57
23.	Inspection and Discovery	59
24.	If You are Pro Se	61
25.	Degree of Clarity in Issues	64
26.	Ethics and Billable Hour	66
27.	Reading the Judge	68
28.	Let's Make a Deal	70
29.	Interlude	72
30.	Ordinance	74
31.	Kumite	77
32.	Cloaking	79
33.	Retainer Disappearance	82
34.	Second Opinion	85
35.	Mary Hartman Second Act	86
36.	Court Ordered Mediation	88
37.	Aha	90

38	Romper Room	93
39	Rug Delivery	96
40	Alienation of Affection	94
41	A Blocked Sewer Explodes	102
42	Contempt of Court	104
43	The Show Cause Hearing for Contempt	106
44	A Model to Manage your Financial Future	110

Chapter One

The Encounter

    A party at a neighbor's house on a private mountain where Benny and Bella live. Bella enters the room and sees a man at the center having a conversation. Armani turns his head and makes eye contact with Bella while opening his stance and turning towards her. He is five foot four and 138 pounds with a thirty-inch waist and has completed a recent triathlon. At age 83 Armani holds the geriatric world record for powerlifting at 462 pounds. His nose is bulbous with tiny, swelling red veins. Armani's head is bald down the center with crops of thin, stringy red hair flowing down. His eyes are large ebony disk and his ears give the appearance of a sprouted vegetable. If one stood next to him, you would get the feeling of standing next to an electrical wire that had fallen from a pole and was emitting sparks. His glance lands and is greeted with a tilted head, crinkled eyes, and widening cheeks. He says welcome to the party, I am a close friend of your neighbor and pleased to meet you. Armani extends his hand and Bella grasp it. Their handshake lingers as their eyes engage. The clasp began dry and as it remained, steam alighted from the center of each palm. The uncoupling drifted frictionless.

W.C.Fields: "I was in love with a beautiful blonde once, dear. She drove me to drink. That's the one thing I'm indebted to her for."

    Bella speaks to her neighbor. "I met your friend and I like him; we have birding in common, and I would like to see him again, what is his email address?"

    "He is staying at my home and joining a group to go birding tomorrow. Here is his email address and phone number."

    Bella's irises enlarge in rooted azure, "I know the birding group he is going with." Her mouth opened, the corners of her lips raised exposing her upper teeth, the clefts along the sides of her nose tightened, eyelids heightened. She raised her forefinger, her shoulders bouncing up and down. "I'll surprise him."

    4:30 a.m.: the parking lot of a wildlife reserve where the birding group meets.

    Bella drives up and sees Armani talking to the group leader. She parks and flings the car door open, takes a deep breath, and explodes towards Armani. Her heart rate hits 120 beats per minute. As she exits her car, she feels a tingle in her inner thighs that speeds her towards Armani.

FIRST STAGE OF DISHARMONY
DISILLUSIONMENT OF ONE PARTY

A. Vague feelings of discontentment, arguments, stored resentments

B. Problems are real but buried

C. Increased distance

D. Fantasy, consideration of pros and cons of divorce

E. Development of strategy for separation

F. Feelings: fear, denial, anxiety, guilt, love, anger, depression, grief

Divorce statistics in the United States: 40 to 50% of first marriages end in divorce, 67% of second marriages and 73% of third marriages.

Do couples uncover the reasons for divorce and adopt strategies and tactics for successful coupling?

Later that night Armani falls asleep.
Rapid eye movements.
He sees himself lying in bed, his pupils are the size of saucers.
The corners of his mouth rose sending a signal to his brain.
His heart rate and blood pressure depict a graph with an upward slope.
He lies in bed covered by a sheet with his head exposed.
On each side of him are an exposed pair of female hands, their faces covered by the sheets.
Armani peeks under the sheets at his double pleasure, sniffing delight.

The sheet above his lower torso begins to rise as though it was a center pole supporting a tent

"I was nauseous and tingly all over. I was either in love or I had smallpox."   Woody Allen

Chapter Two

Adagio (Second Movement)

One week after the union Bella and Armani return to their homes.

Armani emails Bella: it was fun to go birding with you, we had a good time together. Armani's body stirs as he composes this email. His amygdala lights up. This is an ancient part of the brain responsible for primal drives, including sexual arousal. He feels a lower part of his body that has been dormant, swell and stand at attention

Bella: I learned a lot and I feel there is more you can show me. We must stay in touch. When are you returning? Her interior body was without motion.

.Armani: I didn't have plans to come north, but you have changed that. I can train for my next triathlon. I am buying a new red Porsche convertible,we can break it in.

"My love life is terrible. The last time I was inside a woman was when I visited the Statue of Liberty."   Woody Allen

Chapter Three

30 Days after the Encounter

Armani has an explosion of dream states during his waking periods and while asleep: he recalls Tarzan and Jane-the river scene where she is about to be attacked by a crocodile. Armani in loin cloth, dives in the water, turns the croc over and rips his knife through the soft underbelly killing it. Jane's body is limp as he scoops her up, she emits a soft sigh of carnal desire and surrender. Armani cradles her in his arms as they exit the river with their eyes ablaze in the full moon.

Armani calls Bella.

Hi Bella, you have been on my mind. I have been trying to complete a paper on quantum theory dealing with superposition that is due to be presented to the National Science Foundation next month. When I do, I get a flashback of us watching two cardinals mating the last time we met and I felt a spark as I touched your hand.

"I believe people ought to mate for life...like pigeons or Catholics."
Woody Allen

"Oh, I have been thinking about you too. How are you doing?"

"Things have not been going well."

"What do you mean," asked Bella?

"Sex, sex, sex, I am up to here about it (he places his hand under his chin), but I haven't gotten any lately.

The last time I called up my go to hooker she said she had a headache."

"I'm sorry to hear you say that, sweetie. Anything else?"

"It brought back to memory, one time with my first wife, when we were doing it, I found a peeping tom at the window who was booing me."

"That's terrible Armani, is there more?"

"Godfrey Daniels, with a different madame, when I dropped my pants she started to laugh uncontrollably and reduced her price."

"You poor thing."

"Beelzebub, now I know why I have attractive children from my third marriage, and I am thankful."

"Tell me, Armani."

"My wife had a boyfriend who was a male model."

"That's awful, I feel for you."

"Wait, it gets worse, her lover was her psychiatrist. When I asked her how her therapy was going she smiled and said it felt good to lie on the couch.

My doctor said he had tests to run: urine, stool, and semen. I gave him a pair of my briefs."

"Armani, things will be different with me."

"Wait, nothing goes right for me. I was suspicious my first wife was faking orgasms and when I had lunch with three of my friends they told me the same thing."

"Armani, that's a pity. Is there more?"

"Blind dates, no more blind dates, I went out with a woman who had pigtails."

"What do you have against pigtails?"

"They were under her arms."

"I can't believe it Armani."

"You won't believe this: I hold the world record for powerlifting for men between age 80 and 90 and I took one Viagra pill and my tongue got hard."

"Go on Armani, let it all hang out."

"My second wife screams when she has sex. It happened when I walked in on her.

Oh, do I know about oral contraception. I tried to get a woman in bed, and she said no.

It doesn't end. At the beginning of my marriage to my second wife, I asked her if we can have sex twice a day. She said sure, I'll never be home.

If it weren't for pickpockets, I'd have no sex at all.

My wife said, I want to have sex in back seat of the car. I grinned and said let's go. She said I want you to drive."

"Sex at age ninety is like trying to shoot pool with a rope." ~George Burns

Chapter Four

Doings

February.

Bella exchanges emails with Armani. Hello Bella, how are you? You occupy my everyday thoughts and feelings. I will be moving to northern Mexico in July, would you like to visit me?

I don't know, I have to think about it. Send me your address and phone number.

April

Bella has a conversation with her best friend **Lady Pussey Willows.**

Willows noticed her eyebrows and upper eyelids drooped and the corners of her mouth turned downward.

"You seem unhappy, is there something you would like to talk about?"

Bella's shoulders slackened.

"My marriage is not working, I feel alone, we don't do things together."

"Oh, have you thought about counseling?"

"That won't work."

"Why do you stay in the marriage if you are unhappy?"

"It's okay."

Later in April

"Benny, I am booking a trip to Mexico in January, come with me."

"No thanks, Bella, it is not my type of outing. Enjoy yourself with Pussey."

May

"Benny, come with me to Mexico."

"No, love, you go and enjoy yourself."

June

The dinner table.

Benny walks in and sits down.

He looks at Bella attempting to make eye contact, she is sitting at the head of the table, to his right. Bella does not look at Benny and stares straight ahead and says, "you only want to talk about things of your interest." Benny turns his head away and looked up at the ceiling and responds, "okay I'll only talk about things of your interest."

"My love life is like a piece of Swiss cheese; most of it is missing, and, what's there stinks."   Joan Rivers

Chapter Five

Eruption (September)

Bella remarked, "I was talking to our neighbors yesterday."

"Oh, what about," Benny inquired?

"They were talking about how you acted at their Christmas party."

"What do you mean?"

"**Ambrose Wolfinger** said you were trying to hit on his friend."

Bella: "I was there, and I saw it."

Benny had a sensation of a foul, acid like churning in the gut. His jaw muscles went vise-like. The amygdala, an almond shaped brain structure (seat of emotion), searing, glowing, and, vibrating.

"The person he said I was hitting on is in the LBGT community and you know I am not."

Benny pounds the table and thinks.

"This event occurred four years earlier, why is Bella resurrecting it? Wolfinger has been divorced three times and has had bad relationships with women."

The water in the kettle was boiling. It whistled, and spouted steam.

Benny blurted, "I want a divorce."

Bella, eyes moving to the right and upward, in two seconds, said, "OK."

Benny muses, "Bella agreed at once, no suggestion for marriage counseling, as though she anticipated my request, curious."

The following day. At the kitchen table, Benny gives an agreement to

Bella.

She remarks "what is this?"

"Can we agree to keep this simple, inexpensive, and remain friends?", offers Benny. Bella nods as she reads it. "I worked it out that we split the assets, but you will walk away with $50,000 of tax-free income, and I will have $41,000. One other thing, I want to sell real estate and keep the commission's separate from this agreement, is that alright?" Bella responds, "I do not want your money," her voice tearful, and cracking.

They sign the agreement.

Next morning.

"Bella, we have to add to this agreement that you will allow me to keep the money from real estate sales."

"No, I won't sign."

"Marriage is the death of hope" Woody Allen

Chapter Six

The Starting Point

Bella visits attorney **Bonita Broadbottom**. She is in her late seventies, 6 foot seven and 300 pounds. She played substitute lineman for a division 3 college football team. Her dress was haute couture from the Salvation Army rack. A flowing denim skirt that if it was canvas you would think it was a tent. The skirt was two inches below the knees and exposed hairy inverted bowling pin legs. She wore a well ironed white short-sleeve shirt that sported tight, bulging 16-inch biceps. When Bonita spoke her jaw would move with caution, as if she was grinding gravel.

"My husband and I are getting divorced and we signed this agreement and I want to know if you can get me more money."

Bonita reads the paper.

Drat, this is crooked as a dog's hind leg. Bonita jerked back her head and turned it sideways, tilting it. The bluebonnet, with the words stitched in the center "Go Cucamonga," fell off and she made a failed attempt to catch it. Exclaiming, "Lucifer at play again."

There is a bowl of long brown pretzels on Bonita's desk, she takes one out and snorts this is what I can do to this agreement snapping the pretzel in two.

Bella shudders as she watches Bonita's bicep expand as the pretzel is reduced to powder as Broadbottom grinds it into her desk.

At the center of her desk were two fifty-pound dumbbells. On the wall was a photograph of Bonita with the football team of Cucamonga Law School. Bonita shakes her finger at the photograph and says I'll take care of Benny. She gnashes her teeth and twist her lips.

Bonita writes a formula on a piece of paper and hands It to Bella. "This will get you more money." She tilts her head and winks and her bluebonnet falls off her head.

"If my husband decides to contest the divorce, what will your fee be?"

Bonita responds, "about $3,000."

One week later.

Bella: "I went to an attorney about this paper that we signed."

Mars, the bringer of war

"Oh, why?" Benny snapped his head and looked upward to the right. In thought "hmm, there seems to be a **pattern** developing."

"I didn't know if it was fair to split the money in my Roth account. Bonita wrote down this formula and told me she had a way for me to keep more of my Roth account (**Question 1**)."

Benny had done research in how assets are distributed in divorce.

He looked at the formula and said, "Broadbottom doesn't have the necessary information to say that."

Bella asked Benny if he would like to meet with Broadbottom tomorrow. He turned his head away from Bella and nodded.

The next day.

They walk into the Bonita's office and Benny sits down in a chair in front of the desk where Broadbottom sits. Bella has invited me here to discuss our agreement.

Bonita stands up and lifts each dumbbell to press above her head at full extension and growls.

Bonita hands Benny a slip of paper with legal terminology and ask him to sign it.

"Hmm, I know what this means, but let me clarify it." Benny says "what does this mean?"

Bonita responds, "that says I have not taken advantage of you."

"Oh, you already have" responds Benny.

Bonita returns the dumbbells to their resting place and remains towering over Benny. Her lower lip is contorted.

Benny says, "show me in the law where you can get more money for Bella and I will give it to you (Question 2)."

Broadbottom answers, "I can't give you legal advice."

Benny:" okay, Bella knows the questions to ask and I will sit here and be quiet."

Bonita: "no, Mr. Benny you may not, you must leave the office."

Benny rises from the chair and begins pacing.

With a curled upper lip, he points at Bonita.

He turns his head towards Bella, "don't you dare give this person a penny from our marital assets."

He stamps his foot and departs.

Escalation, Stage One

That evening

Benny: "Bella, let's keep this simple and inexpensive. We have two units in our house with separate entrances, I will live downstairs and when the house is sold, we both move. You agree for me to sell real estate and keep the money."

Bella bows her head.

"If you want to stay in the area, I will help you find a house without commission" says Benny.

"Regarding your investment account, I will teach you how to manage it. This will save you thousands of dollars a year in fees."

The next morning

"Here Bella, please sign this agreement giving me permission to keep the money I earn from real estate sales."

"Nope, I won't."

Escalation, Stage Two

Next movement towards divorce

II. EXPRESSING DISSATISFACTION

    A. Expressing discontent or ambivalence to other party

    B. Marital counseling, or

    C. Possible honeymoon phase (one last attempt)
       Feelings: relief (that it's out in the open), tension, emotional roller coaster, guilt, anguish, doubt, grief

Quiz (Do It)

In question 1 above, I believe Bonita had a reliable method to get more money for Bella (true) (false). Support your answer.

In question 2, I believe Bonita's response was reasonable (true) (false).

Defend your answer.

If Broadbottom could demonstrate how she could get more money for Bella in the law, would she have to prove this in Court? (yes) (no). Explain your answer.

How do you rate the manner in which Broadbottom communicated with Benny?

How do you rate the manner in which Benny communicated with Bonita.

"The only time my wife and I had simultaneous orgasms was

when the judge signed the divorce papers." Woody Allen

Chapter Seven

Before the Storm

Bella: "Broadbottom has suggested we hire a mediator to come to a financial agreement."

Benny: "Bonita is a problem. She has made misrepresentations that are contrary to the State Divorce Law. She has catered to your emotions to achieve a good settlement that are outside the boundaries of the law. Her fee is half or less than half, of the market rate. A thoughtful person would seek answers to cut rate professional services. Did you ask for recommendations, a minimum of three, of the most recent clients with divorce issues?"

The next day.

Benny: "I have put together an offer that will give us each about $46,000 in annual income and each of us will receive about $100,000 from the sale of the house. If you reject the offer, litigation follows, and your loss exposure is receiving zero from the sale of the house. In addition, I can document, in writing the cost of your pottery degree with an estimate of $20-$25,000. The Court may require you to pay this."

The next week.

Benny, In an email to Bella.

"You have informed me Broadbottom has stated that the Social Security is not divisible, it follows that she has informed you the same would apply to your annuity. I will not claim these benefits if she can support her argument in the law. You went to her seeking additional money and you wrote down a fixed percentage approach she indicated as an avenue of greater funds for you regarding your Roth account. The second question is, how do you qualify for this approach? We can have a meeting with merit, if Bonita acknowledges in writing she will answer the above two questions. If she responds, that she cannot give me legal advice, you are flushing your money down the toilet bowl."

Quiz

I agree (or disagree) that Broadbottom is appealing to Bella's emotional desire to get more money. Support your answer.

I agree (or disagree) that Benny is asking a reasonable question how Broadbottom will get more money for Bella regarding the Roth account. Back your answer.

I agree (or disagree) Bonita's response to the above question " I can't give you legal advice" is sensible. Is Benny asking for legal advice? Support your answer

Benny does research on the law on how an IRA Roth account is distributed in divorce and finds this can't be done without detailed financial information that Bonita does not have.

Benny believes Bonita is building expectations that she will not be able to deliver. He files a complaint with the State Bar Association (an organization with oversight of attorney ethics) providing the formula Bonita gave Bella showing how she could keep more of her IRA Roth.

The State Bar responded: If it was true Bonita behaved in this way and you could prove it, it would an acceptable attorney practice.

Three days later.

Benny receives an email from Bella offering a settlement.

Bella's IRA Roth account has $225,000 more than Benny's.

She offers that each of them keeps their IRA Roth account.

Benny, in thought, "hmm, State Law indicated these accounts are marital property and should be divided equally unless the parties desire otherwise. Bella is asking me to give her a gift about $112,500. I won't. I get it, Bella wants to keep her entire Roth account and she has hired an attorney to get this done. I know when Bella sets her mind on doing something, she stays with it. I have to protect my interest."

Benny files for equitable distribution through the Court.

"One time I went to a hotel. I asked the bellhop to handle my bag. He felt up my wife!" R. Dangerfield

The Intent of this work is to steer you towards critical thinking and away from emotional reactions. If you apply a minimal effort in analytical thought, you may be able to reduce the large financial drain and emotional torture. The focal point of contested divorce occurs when there is ill-will between the couple that breeds aggression. This hostility is ramped up by the legal process spawning mounting legal bills with emotional ruin. Answer the questions posed in this work and you may be able to save thousands of dollars while reducing emotional devastation. This book offers strategic interventions that will provide great value if <u>you put them into play.</u>

Chapter Eight

The State Bar of Hades

Benny files a complaint with the State Bar that is funded by taxpayers to oversee the ethical behavior of attorneys.

Dear **Countess Maggie Tubbs DePuizzi**, Deputy Counsel
18H0988
    Thank you for your response.
    I submitted copies of the formula Bonita Broadbottom represented to Bella advising her this was a means for her to get a greater share of her investment account.
    Broadbottom did not have financial statements and this was a misrepresentation encouraging Bella to believe Broadbottom could get her more money.
    Your grievance committee (GC) claimed Broad bottom's behavior, if it was true and could be proven, was hunky dory.
    I would like to know if the GC follows the format of the TV game show "Celebrity Charade" in 1979?
    First premise: attorneys are a protected class providing a celebrity status.
    I am curious if the GC operates as a parlor game as follows.
    The chairman (Israel **"Ice Pick Willie"** Bloomer, a ventriloquist) who wears a black bowler hat and has a dummy on his knee named **"Louie Ha Ha."** After the two attorneys who sit on the GC perform their **act**, "Ice Pick Willie" and Louie Ha Ha will conference to decide the winner. "Ice Pick Willie" has a prosthetic arm with three ice picks strapped to it. Louie Ha Ha has several punctures in his eardrums as result of disagreeing with the boss.
    The first attorney, Anthony **"Big Tuna/Joe Batters"** Bruno has a wooden leg that he taps when making an argument representing an African drumbeat. The second attorney, Giuseppe **"Joe Bananas"** Giordano" suffering from Tourette's, used barking and twitching to play out his role.
    My dear Esquires, you have copies of Benny's complaint and Bonita's response indicating it is her ethical responsibility to create ways to get more money for her client without factual financial statements. Bonita is a world-

class poker player and has stated she is employing a tactic known as a semi-bluff that is her ethical charge as an advocate for her clients.

On the docket today we have five complaints. I am the judge and decide who is the victor. The Esquire that wins three of the five bouts will receive two tickets to the Gentlemen's Review on Broad Street featuring **Pussy Galore**. Included is a $10 roll of quarters and two pairs of plastic lined briefs in the event the Esquire soils himself.

Mister Bananas, you will represent the mark, I mean the consumer. I cannot cut you any slack because of your affliction. Between your barking, please enunciate with care. Moreover, you are a basket of massive ticks that makes it hard for me to follow your words. On the table there is a straight-jacket and a gag. You will have a greater chance of success if you put them on. Pussy Galore will be your reward.

Chapter Nine

Rollo La Rue

    Benny and his best friend **Rollo La Rue** (a law professor from New York City), meet for lunch at a restaurant. They sit down and Benny remarks, "I picked up my mail and haven't had time to sort it out. Aha, the usual junk mail and what's this? Hmm ,a letter from my attorney (**Professor Eustace P. McGonagall**)."

    Rollo noticed Benny's upper eyelids and brows rise as his jaw falls wide open as the letter is read. The handshakes as the letter floated downward and he bounces upward. The hands rise to shoulder height with the palms facing the letter. His chest expanded as his lungs froze.

Date	Description	Hours	Cost
4/11/18	Motion to set aside Consent Order	0.2	80.00
4/11/2018	Reviewed motion to Void Consent Order	0.3	120.00
4/12/2018	Organize file	0.1	0
4/13/2018	Reviewed Motion to Cooperate	0.5	200.00
4/18/2018	Telephone call to judge's clerk	0.5	200.00

Date	Description	Hours	Amount
4/18/2018	Reviewed Motions from plaintiff	0.3	120.00
4/19/2018	Responded to email from client	0.1	40.00
4/19/2018	Reviewed emails from plaintiff	0.1	40.00
4/19/2018	Drafted Pleadings Sanctions	0.25	87.50
4/19/2018	Correspondence to mediator	0.1	40.00
4/23/2018	Pleadings for Sanctions	0.5	200.00
4/24/2018	Pleadings Rule 9	1.0	175.00
5/1/2018	Reviewed Motion to Strike		
5/2/2018	Prepared documents to file	0.5	175.00
5/2/2018	Revised Rule 9	0.2	80.00
5/2/2018	Expense Motion to Strike		20.00
5/4/2018	Organize file	0.2	0
5/8/2018	Reviewed Motions by plaintiff	0.1	

Date	Description	Hours	Amount
			40.00
5/18/2018	Reviewed documents	0.3	52.50
5/18/2018	Review plaintiff Motion Separate Property	0.1	40.00
5/18/2018	Responded to emails from client	0.2	80.00
5/18/2018	Expense copies		8.50
5/21/2018	Travel to courthouse	1.0	75.00
5/21/2018	Reviewed Motion 44	0.5	200.00
5/21/2018	Reviewed documents	0.5	210.00
5/21/2018	Prepare for hearing	0.3	120.00
5/22/2018	Reviewed Motion for Clarity	0.2	80.00
5/23/2018	Email client for court date	0.1	17.50
5/25/2018	Prepare for hearing	0.9	360.00
5/28/2018	Prepare for hearing	1.50	600.00
5/29/2018	Prepare for hearing	0.2	

80.00		
5/29/2018	Draft Pleadings	0.4
70.00		
5/30/2018	Prepare for hearing Rule 9	1.0
400.00		
5/30/2018	Prepare for hearing Rule 9	1.0
400.00		
5/31/2018	Attend hearing	1.5
600.50		
6/27/2018	Proposed Orders	2.5
900.00		

Total Due

$6,409.00

QUIZ

In your own handwriting, on a separate piece of paper, write the question, followed by your answer :

1) What have I learned from this chapter-

2) Benny could have prepared for this bill by asking for-

Review each answer as you proceed through this book.

You will <u>empower</u> yourself with each idea.

Chapter Ten

Crucial Tactic

Benny looks up, and, to the right. "Okay, I understand, Bella is making this expensive. The facts show **97%** of divorce cases are not decided by the judge because the couple **runs out of** money.

A settlement is reached that often could have been done quicker with less <u>legal cost</u>. I must consider another way. I will think about representing myself. But wait, what will be the biggest hurdle I must jump? I got it, in order to make good decisions, I need a tool that will provide optimum results.

Detachment

"Use the mind, but never get identified with it. The mind is a good slave, but a very bad master. "The body is wiser." Various works of Osho

Detachment reveals the great paradox of life: in order to achieve a goal, you have to give up your attachment to having it. When you see that the only true source of security is living as your authentic self, then you can let go. What is meant when we speak about detachment?

What Is Detachment?

The dictionary defines detachment as "a state of being objective or aloof."

Being **objective** is powerful in practicing detachment; however, being aloof does not work.

When your emotions are distant, you are severed from your feelings. You are not partaking in decisions and actions.

Emotion is the driving force to **accomplishment**.

Detachment permits profound activity because of the lack of attachment to results. The skill is to behave with confident energetic emotion guided with positive purpose, not tethered to the conclusion.

The ability to **be aware** that you can remove yourself and **reflect, disengage who you are from a desired outcome**, is what detachment is.

Ron W. Rathbun wrote, "True detachment isn't a separation from life, but the absolute **freedom within your mind to explore living**."

Indications of Attachment

When you are linked to a desire, there are feelings that suggest "If I don't have that, I won't be happy." These are feelings/mental states like:

- Anxiety
- Fear
- Anger
- Jealousy
- Hopelessness
- Sadness
- Disconnection
- Pride
- Vanity

Why?

People observe what others want them to be. The person decides what to accept or reject. In our quest for the genuine self, we disconnect from others.

The concepts one uses to define oneself, perform as a barrier. This hinders relationships. **A falsehood regarding happiness is, if you acquire your desires, you are happy.**

The reality is **happiness is the way- not the goal**. If you can acquire objects of desire while avoid being controlled by them, you will have arrived.

What Do We Attach to?

However, you describe yourself may point out an attachment. I am a musician, electrician, student. If the person ceases playing music, the human continues. The individual survives without the role.

How to Detach: 5 Steps

1. Attend to your mind: **What kind of thoughts do you have?** What descriptors are most frequent? What reflection has the greatest association for you? Attachment has an electrical charge. Where do you feel it in your body?. When you pick up this sensation it will provide a doorway to change.

2. **Separate ego from reality**: Your ego might dictate that since you do not get a raise, your future is negative. You are disappointed, that is a thought. **A thought is not reality.** No loss has occurred, since you did not have the money before. Zero has happened except your ideas about your future. Since, the **future does not exist**, nothing has changed.

3. Be comfortable with **uncertainty**: As Deepak Chopra says, "Those who seek security in the exterior world chase it for a lifetime." By letting go of your attachment to the illusion of security, which is really an attachment to the known, you step into the field of all possibilities. You depart the field of Newtonian physics that lives in the world of matter, a particle, and enter the glorious terrain of the quantum garden, pure energy, a wave. This is where you will find true well-being, abundance, and fulfillment.

4. Meditation: **Meditation will rewire your brain**. Sensations and thought impressions that are not productive will be reduced.

5. Be gentle with yourself: **Awareness** comes first **it is okay to have negative feelings because of change difficulty**. You will experience discomfort, your body is wired to repeat the past behavior. When living in this mode you are trapped in your former self. You have sentenced yourself to misery. Your body has found comfort in the known suffering. Long standing hurtful behavior will be replaced with a healthy action practice. **Persist.**

Optimization

In detachment lies the value of uncertainty. In the wisdom of unpredictability lies the **escape from our past**, from what has been. These are the shackles of bygone conditioning. With our consent to walk into the unknown, the field of possibilities expands.

We **release** ourselves to the **innovative mind** that produces boundless opportunities.

I will launch the **Law of Detachment** by the following actions:

1. **Now**, I will adopt detachment. I will permit myself and others the ability to act as they are. I will not dictate my concept of how the world should be. I will not coerce solutions on problems. This will result in new obstacles. I will engage with detached, energetic involvement.

2. **Now**, uncertainty is added to the mix of experience. In my endeavor to accept the unexplored, chaos and disorder, the adventure unfolds.

3. I will travel into the field of potentiality and experience the thrill that will happen when I accept the value of a multitude of options. I will allow the mystery of life to unfold. **I replace fear with adventure.**

Fear and Anger

They are the twin horsemen of annihilation when **critical decisions** are to be made.

A slew of psychological studies report.

1. Where fear breeds uncertainty, anger instills confidence.

2. Angry people are more likely to put the blame on individuals, rather than "society," or fate.

3. Anger makes people more likely to take risks and to minimize how dangerous those risks will be.

4. Researchers have shown that angry people rely more on stereotypes and are more eager to act. It is an activating emotion.

5. <u>**Anger** inhibits our ability to think with **skill.**</u> We are focused on the anger, what has happened to us, what has been done to us. We are not competent to consider other elements related to our anger, and this destroys our ability for effective decision-making. Anger covers up what we think we have lost. It has been shown in the laboratory- brain stress hormones are released that impair sound reasoning.

"I have no idea what I am doing but incompetence has never prevented me from plunging in with enthusiasm."   Woody Allen

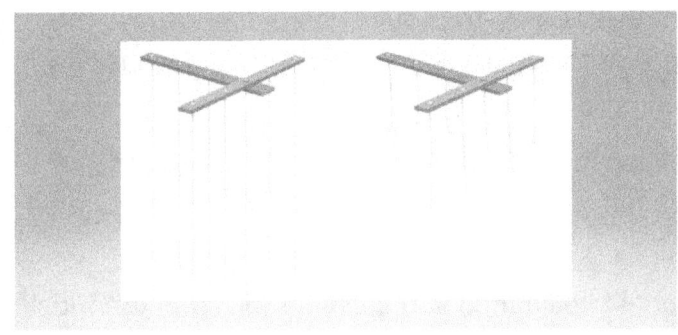

Quiz

1) The most important emotion I must not permit to control my behavior is:

2) The percentage of contested divorces decided by the judge is: and the primary reason is:

Chapter Eleven

Personal Success

There are three types of desirable awareness that may come into play during a contested divorce.

The structure of the legal system has created a process that you will visit Dante's Inferno. Moreover, you will get a glimpse of what Jean-Paul Sartre meant when he exclaimed "hell is other people."

The core mission of this book is to reduce your suffering and provide a platform for you to create a prosperous transition from Hades to Heaven.

The Trinity of Consciousness in the order of significance are: emotional, body and academic. Each of these elements overlap and effect each other.

The level of emotional intelligence you cultivate will carry the most weight in creating successful results. If you permit your emotions to be controlling and consent to your attorney being the captain of the ship, there is a **97%** chance you will throw in the towel before the issue goes to trial because you are drained financially and emotionally.

Body awareness in the form of sensations is the second most critical form of perception. This is intuition, an accurate aspect of intelligence. Pay attention to it. Act on it's advice and the door of wisdom will open. As you travel the abyss of contested divorce you will experience body sensations that obscure Intuitive information. Do not ignore this data. Explore it and see where it leads you.

Begin a consistent daily practice of meditation and you will be on the path to achieving emotional intelligence with body awareness.

The third form of intellect is academic and comprised of learning and critical thinking. This skill will enable you to have clarity regarding the contested divorce process. You will have the ability for effective involvement In the decisions that will be required where you become a partner with your attorney and in control of the purse strings.

The degree in which you apply the above three forms of intelligence will have a direct bearing on reducing your legal bills.

The same principle applies as respects your recovery and advancing to a successful continuation of your life. Further, you may be able to avoid the disaster of a second failed marriage.

Chapter Twelve

The Most Important Question You Can Ask.

You believe your lawyer is experienced in contested divorce.

Dear attorney, the research indicates more than **90%** of contested divorces <u>do not</u> go to trial. The main reason is people run out of money to pay lawyer fees. **Why is my case going to be different?** Please tell me you know about this. The lawyer responds: "each case is different, couples have different needs, and, uncovering the assets could be a problem. Contested divorces are complicated with detailed procedural requirements."

Before you can get an accurate understanding of your attorney, you must get the correct comprehension of yourself. If you do not understand yourself, you will make errors in the attempt to comprehend another. When we add the ingredients of fears and desires that are rife in contested divorce, our judgment becomes hazy, fostering missteps.

If you pay attention to the lawyer's response, you will notice it is not an answer.

What does **your gut tell you** about the attorney's answer?

How do you feel about it?

Trust your <u>intuition</u>. It is a valuable tool to provide questions and answers.

Create yourself in the role of an observer. Review the thoughts and emotions you feel as though they were occurring in another person.

Is the lawyer being straightforward with you?

If you decide to pay for the services of this person, it is probable, you will find what most people do. You will run out of money and get an amount of assets that could have been received sooner.

In order to respond to above with focus and clarity, you must not permit your emotions to become involved. Please, do not be timid in asking the question.

Please be mindful, you are paying the bills and this person is required to provide skill and value to you.

If you take action on this chapter, you will save thousands of dollars with less **emotional pain**.

Quiz

1) The chance my case will end because I run out of money is-

2) What actions can I take to avoid above:

"Life is full of misery, loneliness, and suffering - and it's all over much too soon."   *Woody Allen*

The second demanding question to ask your attorney is- will you outline a plan to achieve a fair result in the shortest time possible?

Please write down the answer and keep it as a guide.

Chapter Thirteen

How to Choose an Attorney

This is of the greatest importance in choosing a person to litigate.

An unfortunate choice will lead to poor performance and possible replacement.

When you replace an attorney you start a relationship anew, time and money has been squandered.

Here is where your gut may be the most valuable asset.

Do you feel comfortable with this person?

Is this individual sensitive to your financial and emotional needs?

When you meet this person the first time, it is critical to be relaxed, not under stress.

If you experience a good amount of tension, your perceptions will be blurred and your decision compromised.

The lawyer's people skills are of utmost importance.

This person will be communicating with another attorney, the judge, and perhaps, experts. You want someone who is flexible and observant. Many lawyers are on automatic pilot. They react with a robotic response in a situation they have had experience with. Avoid this person. Look for someone who pays attention and makes adjustments.

Search for an attorney who will represent your interests with an effective, cordial approach.

Concept: instruct your lawyer to look for opportunities to reduce aggression. At each juncture of the case, there will be chances to limit aggression. This does not mean one gives up one's rights, the purpose is to keep communication going based on logic and law, not emotion. Your lawyer need not respond with a hostile attitude when faced with this type of action. Alternatives should be explored, to prevent runaway combativeness.

You should be transparent with this person. Do not withhold or distort information. If you do, this could have negative consequences. Untoward occurrences have a way of snowballing.

Find an attorney who will welcome your participation.

This will result in quicker and better outcomes for all parties.

If the lawyer wants to take full control, look elsewhere. Ask the lawyer if this person is willing to help you manage the legal cost.

Request if a limited scope service can be done.
Inquire which task can be done by you.
Which clerical activities can be eliminated or reduced?
How many cases has this person litigated that have similar details to yours?

What percentage of their cases are decided by the judge?

Will this person exercise judicious care in motion practice?

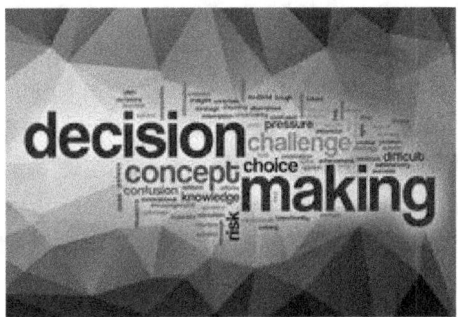

"Posting calorie counts on the menu is like a girl tattooing the number of STDs she has on her vagina. Everyone close enough to read those stats is already committed to that bad decision."   Daniel Tosh

If you permit emotions to influence your choices, you will create negative chemical reactions that are based on neurology. This has been proven in the science laboratory. The results will be unhealthy choices.

Quiz
The reason I chose this attorney is:

Chapter Fourteen

A Critical Skill

Stress Management

Goenka retreat, Jessup, Georgia, there is a meditation hall where 50 people are sitting on cushions. The room is divided in two with 25 men on one side and 25 women on the other. They sit for one hour and are requested not to move or break their posture. I am sitting and I observe my fellow meditators. The mark of an accomplished meditator is being able to sit with a straight spine for 60 minutes. After about 40 minutes I notice the men are beginning to change positions. After five more minutes they start to leave the room. I glance at the ladies; I see perfect posture without movement and wonder what's going on. After another 15 minutes more men leave, and other men change their postures. The women are statute perfect. Before the hour finishes five men have left the hall and seven men have broken their position. Sitting for this period of time causes discomfort or pain. What was special or different about the women since they didn't experience a breakdown under a stressful situation? Later I inquired of the manager, why were women superior meditators? There was laughter and he responded, "when things get tough, women find a way, men run."

This is critical information for both sexes. Many states require mediation. This is an attempt to have the couple settle based on agreement, not law or numbers.

If you are a man, and, you do not heed what follows, you will have non-optimum results. Despite having an attorney to consult, mediation is a high stress experience. If the couple has strong negative emotions for the other, the **emotions will blind you**.

Stress is defined as change where you may have little control and a large amount of uncertainty.

Psychological studies indicate that men and women manage stress in a different manner.

Men reflect less concern about handling stress and believe they are doing a good job.

Women express they have great concern in this matter and are not doing enough. Females have multiple strategies to cope with stress: time with friends and family, praying, religious services, getting a massage and seeing a mental health professional.

Men resort to exercise and drugs to reduce stress. Men believe stress has little impact on their performance or health. This may explain why they devote little attention to the negative effects of stress on their behavior. Cortisol levels increase during the buildup of stress.

This will impair cognitive aspects of decision-making. It follows, that if the male is less successful in coping with stress, he will be at a disadvantage when opposing a female.

Moreover, emotions such as fear and anger will spike during a disquieting experience. Other emotions such as guilt or shame, or whatever may surface. These harmful chemical reactions will compromise your ability to make a good decision. The clear message here is you want a **competent female lawyer**. She will deliver better results than most males.

The methods I have chosen to reduce stress are:

"The trouble with the rat race is, even if you win, you're still a rat."
Lily Tomlin

Chapter Fifteen

Collaborative Law Model

Each person hires an attorney to act as a consultant.

The lawyer is to act as a guide for the client.

The task of each representative is to arrive at a settlement the couple believes fair.

The negotiation is directed towards balance, not for one person to take advantage of the other.

Laws and legal concepts need not be introduced into the discussion.

If the couple can reach an agreement independent of the law, that works.

If they want to divide the assets according to the law, the lawyers can provide the necessary information to settle. If there is disagreement with an issue, it can be set aside and addressed at a later date. The lawyers are not to introduce argument into the process. Their assignment is to avoid confrontation. Not to give their clients the impression they are working to give them a better deal.

If this approach does not bear fruit, perhaps there will be areas of agreement and a narrowing of the disputes. Another critical value may have been produced. The emotions of the parties may have been tempered by the concept of collaboration. If the emotions can avoid the boiling point, successful movement is possible. When aggression and anger are limited, progress can be obtained.

The people can divide the assets as they choose. The goal of this approach is to avoid anger and have them arrive at a settlement that they can both live with, to prevent litigation. If agreement cannot be reached, each party will have a reasonable understanding of the issues at hand that may be able to prevent the cost of expensive, extensive litigation.

Rage is the most destructive emotion of the mind. We waste energy when we become angry. Being angry uses up as many as 37 muscles that tense and tighten. In turn, smiling only uses up seven muscles. When we have to use more of our muscles, we are spending more of our energy.

Quiz
The value of the collaborative law approach is:

What is the difference between love and marriage?
Love is blind and marriage is an eye opener.

Chapter Sixteen

Goals

How you build your expectations has great consequence in negotiation or trial performance. What you will attain will be subject to the arbitration skills of your lawyer, this person's talent in litigation, the law and chance.
Write what your desired achievements are with specifics.
If they are money issues relating to assets describe them in detail.
At once produce all relevant financial statements including other assets such as real estate or other.

Do not seek revenge against your other. This will cloud your mind.

Do not create goals that you believe may be unrealistic. This will complicate and hinder your success.

If you believe an objective may be unreasonable, discuss it.

Forecast and the Law
1) Discuss where the law supports your assumptions.
1) Examine how your desires could be denied.
2) Inquirer what you attorney has produced in similar situations.
3) What unexpected event may occur? How do you deal with it?
4) Discuss areas where you are exposed to loss and estimate the amount. What is the probability of these losses?
5) What is your lawyer's track record with this judge?

Quiz
My most meaningful <u>goal</u> is:

Sir, I reviewed this case with great care, and I've decided to give your wife $275 a week. That's great your honor, that's more than fair. And every once in a while, I'll throw her a few extra bucks.

Chapter Seventeen

Detailed Itemized Bill

You go to an automobile repair shop; you will receive an estimate in detail for the proposed work. Detailed means each individual service and part installed. Your attorney tracks the billing by computer and can provide you a statement that discloses each charge. Request a statement on a weekly basis, this will make you aware of the cost of the service.

Do not be shy or timid in discussing the lawyer's charges and fees to you. These are negotiable based on agreement between you and the attorney. Most lawyers charge a flat rate per hour. Each case will differ in complexity and difficulty. Inquire with your situation fits in. If your conditions are of a simple nature, you may be able to negotiate a lower fee. Do not be apprehensive in this regard. Lawyers believe when you engage them in equitable distribution, you relinquish management control.

"Older women are best because they always think they may be doing it for the last time." — *Ian Fleming*

Chapter Eighteen

Cost of Divorce

Divorce has the potential to **financially devastate you**.

When it comes to you and your case, there are six principles your divorce lawyer should tell you from the first meeting.

Divorce is not as low cost as you think.

Ask your attorney to give you a statement estimating the total cost of the process detailing it by each stage. This estimate should include supplemental expenses such as expert witnesses or stenographers.

The final price of your divorce will depend on the issues you need to resolve and whether your case is settled out of Court or litigated in front of a judge.

Having an estimate cost of each stage of the process will be helpful regarding decisions of settlement offers.

Hiring an accountant early can save you money later

If alimony is an issue, you should consider hiring an accountant at the outset of the case.

Most states weigh financial income and expenses during the marriage as a factor in determining alimony when the marriage dissolves. While you might generally know where your money went during the marriage, an accountant can remove all doubt often discerning earnings and expenditures to the penny. This can narrow the range of a settlement for both parties and in many cases, remove the need for further litigation on the issue, resulting in further savings.

Hiring a joint expert will simplify the process. A joint accountant does not take sides but objectively lays out the financial picture of the parties. While the cost might seem high, the reality is that it may save you both time and money in legal fees.

Hire an attorney who provides value for their services.

Look for a counselor that will help you analyze your divorce as a financial transaction. Your goal is to walk away from your divorce in the best possible financial position. The value received from litigating must exceed the costs of the effort. Spending ten dollars in extended litigation to "win" five dollars is a **failure**.

See a financial planner if you stand to receive substantial assets.

If you have been married for some time, you and your spouse probably have assets that will need to be divided. These assets can generate income. Other assets have expenses that need to be managed.

If you were a stay-at-home spouse, you may find yourself in control of substantial assets that you are not equipped to manage effectively.

You may find yourself in settlement negotiations where part or all of an alimony claim is waived in exchange for additional assets.

These conversations can lead to win-win settlements for both parties, remember that your counselor is not a trained financial planner. In a high-asset cases, you need help from a financial expert to properly value settlement possibilities.

Be wary of attorneys that charge by the hour.

You pay for hours worked by your attorney, regardless of the value provided.

Ask more questions of the attorney who charges by the hour. Consider setting weekly reviews to ensure that the process is on track, and that you are **receiving value** for the hours worked.

Encourage your counselor to discuss with the other attorney if they can agree on a process to minimize cost.

Please ask your attorney about alternative fee arrangements and value billing **models**. See if your attorney has enough confidence in their process that he or she can quote a flat fee for a segment of the case.

Seek emotional help

Divorce is **emotionally** and psychologically **traumatizing**.
Yet you are about to be asked to push those emotions aside so that you can make clear-headed rational decisions about your financial future.

Seek the help of counselors and other independent parties who are trained in helping you through a difficult and emotional time.

A divorce coach may be a valuable investment.

What does a divorce coach do?

Consider marriage counseling instead of divorce

1) Preparation for divorce
1) Knowledge of the system
2) Choosing between mediation, collaboration, or litigation
3) Select and work with a lawyer

4) Create a cost-effective divorce team
5) Saving time while reducing cost
6) Preparing for mediation
7) Court preparation
8) Preparing for the positive adventure of your new life

Conclusion

A noxious divorce can destroy you and your spouse financially.

An intelligent divorce can lead to win-win results for both parties.

Enabling them to move on towards brighter and better futures.

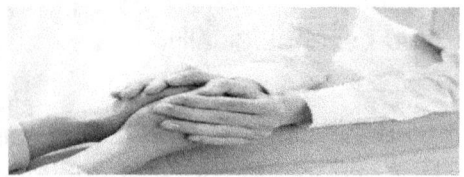

Do I have a reliable estimate of the total cost of litigation and am I receiving value:

Chapter Nineteen

Cost Reduction Strategy

Benny and Rollo meet for lunch.
Rollo removed a gavel from a royal blue, velvet pouch.
Benny shakes his head with rapidity.
Rollo raises the gavel and pounds it into the top of a napkin holder and a slew of napkins dribble out.

You have come to me because of your interest to represent yourself. This is the most difficult task for you to accomplish with good results.

First, before you replace, or change your attorney, have your name added as co-counsel. This will enable you to provide input, if you decide to maintain representation.

The following ideas will reduce your <u>legal cost</u>s in the event you maintain counsel.

1. Divorce can be a financial devastation.
2. Often one or both parties may have deep unhealed **emotional wounds** that have been exposed in this process. It is critical that each person assesses their emotional state. If **anger** or other negative emotions are controlling, the person will be unable to focus with clarity on the issues at hand. The sole outcome will be poor decisions. In addition, ineffective decision-making in the early stages increases the probability of awful choices later. One is exposed to a compounding effect.
3. If you have questions about your emotional stability, find a competent professional that will support you through a process that may bring out your worst **emotional fears.** If your judgment is compromised, it will lead to larger legal bills and suffering.
4. An attorney will be aware of your emotional involvement and may not counsel on its dangers. This will result in a bigger bill.
5. An attorney who is concerned with your needs, will suggest you seek professional help, if he (or she) notices your negative emotional state. <u>Do not</u> wait for this. It is your job to be **aware** of your emotional state and take **corrective action.**
6. Hence, the most demanding decision you make, is who you choose to

represent you. This person should have the training, experience, and technical skills required. The challenge is few clients have the ability to choose an effective attorney. They rely on a referral from a friend who is lost as much as they are. Another question is how do you feel about this lawyer as a human being? What does your intuition tell you? This is another occasion where you do not want your emotions to enter, because the results will not satisfy you.

7. The hard-inconvenient truth is you must be involved and the deeper you are the better your results will be.

8. They're are lawyers who will understate the total cost of litigation. They do not want to frighten you and lose a client. The cost will be determined by the number and complexity of issues in dispute. The opposition of your other will have a great influence on the cost. It is best to agree on as many items as possible to avoid the attorneys trying to upstage one another.

9. Inspection and discovery where each party request documents and ask questions of the other party, maybe the most expensive part of the litigation. Often a good part of this information never sees the judge's desk. You should instruct your lawyer to limit this process to vital subject matters alone. Moreover, court stenographers can be expensive.

10. Litigation does not move in a straight line. The fortunes of each party will shift during the process. Demand a cost assessment at each stage of the development. This is decisive if there are settlement offers made enabling a cost-benefit analysis. Your goal is to receive value for your participation. This demands an active review of what you pay and what you get.

11. The task is not to punish your other but to arrive at an equitable settlement. If you seek revenge, you will dig two graves, one for you and one for your X.

12. If alimony or child support is involved, consider hiring an accountant. This will simplify matters and be less expensive with both parties represented. Their job can be to enumerate the assets accumulated during the marital period as well as premarital monies. You can get an estimate of what the accountant would charge versus what the attorneys will charge.

13. Beware if the attorney tells you they will destroy your other in Court. Often divorce action causes the worst of human behavior. The negative message of this lawyer is they are seeking your permission to run up the legal bills.

14. If there are assets involved such as real estate, stocks, bonds or other

securities, seek the counsel of a financial planner. Do not go to a financial advisor of a brokerage firm whose livelihood is maintained by sales. Few of these salespeople will place your interest first.

15. Your lawyer will write motions that are request to the Court to do an activity. What is the cost of the motion? What does it do? Is it worth it? What happens if the motion is not productive? What is the probability the motion will succeed? You do not want this person to write ineffective or unnecessary motions.

16. <u>Do not</u> contact your attorney unless it is an absolute necessity. You will be charged in every instance. Do not discuss the personal behavior of your other with your lawyer unless it is of a legal nature.

The best time to consider the cost and value of legal representation, is **before** you hire an attorney.

The intention of this book is to encourage you to use it before you engage an attorney and hire the lawyer as a **coach**, if the battle begins.

If you <u>do not</u> adopt this valuable suggestion, you will find yourself as the photograph below. Hamstrung by your **emotions** and bleeding money.

Quiz
The tactics that will save me the most amount of money are:

Chapter Twenty

Mediation

The mediator explains the process and its confidential nature. Each party explains their position. The mediator begins creating possible solutions. With the mediator being a neutral person, negotiations begin to arrive at a solution that satisfies both parties.

What should I bring with me to the Mediation session?

You will be provided with worksheets to fill out regarding your assets, liabilities and budgets. Please fill these out prior to your appointment. You should come to the mediation with as much information regarding your dispute as possible. In addition to the information on your forms, this can include bank statements, financial statements, tax returns, real estate valuations, medical records, etc. The more information that the parties and the mediator have the greater the chance of a successful mediation session.

Should an attorney attend the Mediation session with me?

In a Court ordered mediation, the parties' attorneys must attend the mediation. If the issue is not the subject of a lawsuit, it is up to the parties whether to have attorneys present. There are pros and cons. If attorneys are present, they can help clarify your legal rights as well as advise you on the strengths and weaknesses of your legal position. This can be helpful in the negotiation process. If both parties have attorneys present, the attorneys can draft a binding agreement for the parties to sign at the end of the mediation session. It is not, however, necessary that attorneys be present. In some cases, it is beneficial for the parties to communicate directly rather than through their attorneys. This depends on the nature of the issue. For instance, it is often beneficial for families, separating couples, or business partners to attempt to communicate directly.

This allows the parties to create a solution that is based more on their individual needs rather than what they are "entitled" to under the law or what would have been the result had the issue gone to Court.

Will I leave Mediation with a legally binding agreement?

If both parties have attorneys present, the attorneys can draft a legally binding agreement for the parties to sign at the end of the mediation. If attorneys are not present, the mediator can provide the parties with a Memorandum of Understanding that sets forth the terms they have agreed upon in mediation. The parties must have one of their attorneys put these terms into a binding settlement agreement.

Can an outside professional give advice during a Mediation session?

Yes. In fact, outside professionals such as CPAs, business valuators, child therapists, parenting coordinators, and realtors, can provide advice allowing the parties to make informed decisions during the process. These professionals can attend the mediation session with the parties. During mediation, these professionals can participate as neutral experts and can be relied upon by both parties – thereby avoiding the expense of each side having to hire their own expert.

Do the parties go through a Mediation session in the same room?

Joint mediation sessions are preferable as they allow parties to hear each other's needs and concerns. However, the need for separate sessions arises quite often – especially when parties don't feel comfortable sharing information with each other.

How long will Mediation take?

The length of a mediation session depends on the intricacy of the dispute. A simple dispute can be mediated in as little as two hours or less while a multi-layered dispute may take 10 hours or more. Parties to divorce and custody mediation may choose to conduct the mediation session all at once or in 2-3-hour intervals until the issues are settled.

A strong recommendation is made if there is anger or hostility between the couple or there is a large amount of assets in dispute, sessions be limited to 2 hours.

This will reduce the likelihood of stress-induced decisions that will be regretted.

Can the Mediator give me legal advice or provide me with legal services?

A mediator cannot act as an attorney while conducting a mediation. Therefore, the mediator may not give legal advice or provide legal services as part of their services. There is an advantage to hiring a mediator who is an attorney: they can be better equipped to guide your negotiations with proper questions and considerations.

Critical Behavior-<u>DO NOT SIGN</u> an agreement in the first session.... A memorandum should be drafted indicating in detail a proposed settlement. The reason for this is that the settlement will be filed at the Court, signed by a judge, and become valid and enforceable. The mediation process is laden with massive stress and your decisions will be subject to the stress. Under these conditions, the probability of a poor decision increases unless you wait for at least 24 hours. You can use this time to consult with your attorney, review your <u>goal</u>s and affirm they are being met.
This approach is independent of the law, what you could achieve in Court. The parties agree to what they believe fair and satisfies each one. If you go this route, do not abandon the guidelines above. The task is to satisfy your needs and is up to the couple to decide the method.
You can mediate or go to Court. It is important to remain with the chosen approach and be aware, if you're deviating. If you are, search for the reason. If it is emotional in nature, this is a warning sign. When emotion creeps into your decision-making, you will falter. Moreover, you may be blind to the effect your **emotions** are having at the moment.
The goal of litigation would be to achieve what your attorney has informed you can be obtained in Court.
With full disclosure of all financial information, investment accounts, real estate and other assets, this figure should be obtainable and accurate. Next you decide if this is the number you want or if you want to apply

flexibility by being generous.

If you decide to be generous, put a number on your generosity, example-10% of what you could get in Court. If you go beyond this number, be aware of it and ask yourself why.

There may be issues in your case where it is unclear if you can get money or the amount it would be. Ask your attorney for an estimate of this amount and the probability of you getting it.

You may decide to negotiate this aspect and by putting a number on it you are better prepared, and, can make a **sound conscious decision**.

Mediation Checklist

Method [ ] obtain what Court proceedings would provide
1. Investment accounts, divide by marital and separate, total each.
What is the figure you desire regarding the marital investment accounts?
Amount-   do you have flexibility in this figure? How much?
2. Real estate, what dollar amount do you want? Amount-is this negotiable?
3. Other assets, itemized. Apply the same technique as above.

When you decide to obtain what is achievable in Court you should stay within these guidelines and not deviate without good reason. Stress will mount and this will increase the probability of your breakdown. Do not crumble, every hour take at least a ten-minute break, meditate, exercise or stay mentally active in an unrelated subject (music, movies, literature).

The value of I have received from mediation is:

Do not sign the agreement if you have important reservations. If there are issues that do not satisfy you, negotiate to have these modifications included in the agreement. Once the agreement is signed by the judge, both parties will have a legal obligation to comply.

She began to wonder if they were beyond mediation.

"I'm taking Viagra and drinking prune juice - I don't know if I'm coming or going."
Rodney Dangerfield

Chapter Twenty One

Stipulation

Stipulation occurs when both lawyers agree on a subject matter. It can be an aspect of law, definition or mathematics.

Instruct your lawyer to search where stipulation can be agreed upon.

Place an emphasis on this request.

If attorneys can collaborate, work together, to stipulate as many issues as possible, the cost of inspection and discovery will be reduced.

If there is a trial, it will be streamlined with less objections to evidence.

The act of simplifying and shortening a trial reduces legal expense.

If the attorneys become gladiators in the coliseum, the couple will be paying a high-ticket price.

If your lawyer must respond with aggression, hold this person to successful results.

Being offensive, without worthwhile results, invites a counterattack. And so on, and so forth. The field is full of blood, producing failure.

Chapter Twenty-Two

Productivity of Motions or other actions as it relates to Cost

1) When your lawyer produces a motion, discuss the purpose of the motion.
2) Does this purpose satisfy your goal?
3) Will your other oppose the motion?
4) What is the total cost of the motion?
5) Can the Court decide the motion on the papers alone, without oral argument? Your lawyer should be able to reduce to writing the required arguments. In doing this you will have limited your <u>legal cost</u>. If oral argument is required by the judge, ask for an exception. If the judge reads the motion before the oral argument, this person will have made it's decision before you enter the Courtroom. If critical, relevant information can be added to the motion, it may be worth the cost of these legal fees.
6) If it is a different legal form, apply the same reasoning as above.
7) Ask the lawyer what is your experience with these types of motions with this judge?
8) If the motion offers case law, is it on point?
9) If it is a brief, apply above criteria.
10) The above data will provide an effective measure of your lawyer's performance.

Response to Opponent

What does your lawyer expect the responses of their opponent will bring?

Does your attorney have a countermeasure?
What liability are you exposed to by the response of your other?
Quantify the liability and determined if it is acceptable.
How can this exposure be managed?

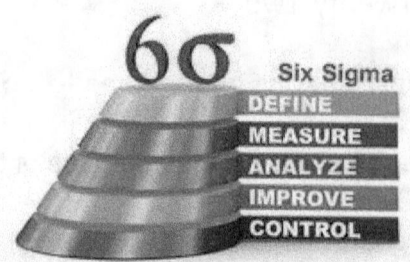

Quiz
The following motions by my attorney have not been effective:

"I've got all the money I'll ever need. If I die by 4:00."-Henny Youngman

Chapter Twenty-Three

Inspection and Discovery

You have executed a summons and complaint and the defendant has answered.

This is a process where data and depositions are gathered for possible presentation at trial. This is the mother lode for litigators. The action may never get to trial, and this data mining was a complete waste of legal expense. Often inspection and discovery are drawn out. If the case goes to trial, repeatedly a scant amount of the data will be relevant. Moreover, by objection, it may be omitted as evidence.

This is where you may have a significant advantage if you are pro se, a prime weapon is to apply excruciating detail and depth in the search for evidence that will support your position. If you do not believe you are up to this job, consider hiring a lawyer to lay the groundwork.

If you are going to hire an attorney, direct this person to include you in all filings and other activities.

It is your option to choose how active you decide to become.

The greater control you exercise the better your results will be with less cost.

When you require your lawyer to include you as co-counsel you are indicating you have input into the process.

This puts this person on notice, they are a guide, not a master.

Quiz
The ways my attorney made an effort to minimize the cost of inspection and discovery:

"I told my wife she's lousy in bed; she went out to get a second opinion."
Rodney Dangerfield

Chapter Twenty-Four

If you are pro se

This is a **strong recommendation** that you <u>do not</u> represent yourself unless you hold the requisite talents. Few people do but this book can provide training, if you possess the necessary skills beforehand. At risk is your emotional involvement that can be minimized but not eliminated.

As the stress accelerates your performance will deteriorate without the proper foundation and training. The main focus of this book is to open your eyes to the process.

This will enable you to protect your interest that could be a swift, reasonable resolution, without a financial fiasco and **emotional demolition.**

If you decide to represent yourself, this book is the manual how to do it with success.

However, without the required skills, you will make errors that may be costly.

The first, most vital ingredient, is **emotional intelligence.**

Decision-making is based on facts and law, not your desires

If you have deep emotional unhealed wounds, they may bubble up to the surface.

Feelings of **fear or anger** will inhibit good choices and will be self-destructive.

Dwelling on the shortcomings of your spouse and the failure of the marriage will hinder your performance.

If you can isolate your emotions from the task at hand, it may be okay to proceed.

You may consider professional psychological support to enable you to go forward.

The law has many procedural requirements where attention to detail is utmost.

Are you a detail person?

Throughout law two words dominate, **"sound reasoning."**

This is found in two ways, logical arguments and trial court findings. Appellate decisions are the greatest teacher.

How to deal with attorneys if you are pro se

Nonlawyers who attempt this arcane field of competition are viewed with a polite disrespect by lawyers.

The attorneys are not incorrect since they have met few people that have a comprehension of the law and the complicated procedures.

If you decide to go it alone, despite the warnings in this book, you may have a quiet advantage.

However, have you passed the test outlined?

If you have answered yes, it is suggested that you proceed with caution.

When you do legal research, do it again, on the same matter and do it again.

Form an understanding of the case law as it relates to your situation.

Search for the most recent findings as this may uncover a trend in judicial reasoning.

What are the latest statutory changes as they relate to your case?

When you believe you have a clear understanding of the case law have a consultation with a lawyer to confirm your beliefs. It is critical to find where your thinking is correct and of greater importance where it incorrect.

Judicial findings have an amazing consistency. The judges call it "sound reasoning" and there is little digression when they view similar facts of the case and the law. If material facts differ from case to case, rulings may depart, however, the underpinning is "sound reasoning." If your conditions have a great similarity to previous settings, the cake has been baked except for the whip cream.

This is where your poker playing ability will be tested and your opponents. The superior poker player will have an advantage because the opponent will lack clarity and courage regarding the issues.

Moreover, you are playing in a new schoolyard with your opponent being superior in this regard. Fear may well up in your tummy. Your decision-making capabilities will deteriorate. You may look for the exit.

"Never, never, never give up."
Winston Churchill

Remain calm, breathe with deep breaths, experience, do not react.

The silent edge you may possess is your opponent will deem you to be incompetent.

Your opposite will believe you present no risk of loss.

This person subconscious will rumble: "I had to qualify for law school, two years to graduate and pass the State Bar exam. Tens of thousands of dollars invested to produce a master of critical thinking and a dynamo litigator.

My overwhelming firepower makes this an unequal contest."

Guaranteed, your adversary is overconfident.

This presents an exposure to loss.

Nonetheless, you must possess the tools and the executory skill to pull the trigger.

Chapter Twenty-Five

Degree of Clarity in the Issues, Case Law, Rulings, Trends

What is the complexity of your situation?
Do you have issues that have a clear definition in the law?
If the disputes are not well-defined, what is the degree of ambiguity?
How does this affect your risk exposure to financial loss?
Do you have solid evidence to support your view?
How has the judge ruled in similar cases?
If your case is straightforward, how can it be directed with force and economy?
Quickness to get to the issues on the table will reduce your expense and emotional negativity.
Ask your attorney to suggest means to move the process with speed.
Court procedures have great rigidity but can be modified with effort.
You and your attorney must be involved to create change.
This positive change is a direct benefit to you.
Does your case have aspects that do not yield to research findings?
Since few actions are decided by the judge. There may be a host of gray areas with nebulous possible outcomes. Do they exist and how does your lawyer address them?
Do you face exposure to loss in these gray areas?
Or does your opponent?
What is the track record of your lawyer in cases similar to yours as it relates to cost and results?
This is a test of the poker playing ability of your attorney.
In poker the winning player must outperform their opponent in calculation and execution.
The same process occurs in chess.
Law extols it's image in the search for truth and justice.
However, the attorney with the superior poker playing skills has a huge advantage.
How does your lawyer and the opposing attorney rate in this category?

You can estimate this by a review of the overall efficiency of your attorney regarding performance using the guidelines suggested in previous chapters.

VUCA-Volatility, Uncertainty, Completeness, Accountability

Quiz

How has my lawyer made it clear to me where I stand in the process:

"Is sex dirty? Only if it's done right."   Woody Allen

Chapter Twenty-Six

Ethics and Billable Hours

An ethical requirement of the State Bar is the attorney to be competent.

The issue with this is that there is a boundless sea of what competency is.

It may not include a cost reducing approach to your case.

Legal procedure is tedious and comprehensive.

It is been done this way since the early English Courts.

An opening question for an attorney should be what can you do to keep the cost at a minimum?

Do not accept that there are requirements to be met beyond this person's control.

You are putting this person on notice that there is no carte blanche.

The judge has wide discretion about what is required in the Court.

A prime example will be the calendar call.

The parties meet with the judge in the Courtroom to schedule an agenda.

This can be done via a conference call.

Rather than have the lawyers charge for travel time, waiting time in Court and agreeing with the other party, each attorney can be contacted by the judge's clerk and the proceedings fixed.

Each transaction can be accomplished in less than 10 minutes producing a vast reduction in <u>legal cost</u>s.

Quiz

These are the ways my lawyer has used to minimize my cost:

Chapter Twenty-Seven

Reading the Judge

A critical aspect of your case will be how this person interprets the judicial landscape.

There are judges who have a narrow viewpoint on procedure and the law. This could be favorable for you but that would depend on the details of your case. This judge may rule with strict compliance to procedure and practice. Other judges may take a top-down approach, look at the bigger picture, and place greater emphasis on substance as opposed to form. A third type of justice would be a combination of the above two. This type of judge creates problems and opportunities. If you can discern how this person interprets individual situations, you will do well.

Ask your attorney to assess their skill in anticipating the judge's rulings. What has been their experience with the judge?

The ability to do this could have a large impact on your result.

Hannah: Excessive masturbation?

Mickey: You gonna start knockin' my hobbies?   Woody Allen, Hannah & her sisters

Chapter Twenty-Eight

Let's Make a Deal

The format of *Let's Make a Deal* involves selected members of the studio audience, referred to as "traders," making deals with the host. In most cases, the trader will be offered something of value and given a choice of whether to keep it or exchange it for a different item.

The program's defining game mechanism is that the other item is hidden from the trader until that choice is made. The trader does not know if they are getting something of greater value or a prize that is referred to as a "zonk," an item chosen to be of little or no value to the trader.

The negotiation practices of lawyers are similar to "Let's Make a Deal."

They are playing poker and the chips are your money.

The lawyers bargain back and forth each with knowledge of the relative strength and weakness of their clients position pursuant to the law.

The client is in a fog and blind to the game being played.

The greater the passionate involvement the spouse has, the deeper the haze.

The couple is clueless to the value of the poker chips. In the TV show, the contestant is offered a deal and presented an option for possibly a better deal. This person cannot make a decision based on logic because logic does not exist and emotion rules. This tracks with what occurs when two attorneys negotiate a settlement. The couple lacks the information they need to make a rational choice. This is what happens in contested divorce. This goes on until the pain of unrelenting legal bills overcomes the couple.

Quiz
My lawyer has explained to me the strengths and weaknesses in my negotiation in the following ways:

"I remember the first time I had sex – I kept the receipt."
Groucho Marx

Chapter Twenty-Nine

Interlude (October)

Bella phones Counselor Bonita.

"Hello Bonita, I have been thinking about what happened in your office the other day."

"Oh, Bella what do you mean?"

"I hired you to get Benny to give me all of my Roth account."

"I know but your husband came in here and tried to push me around. He ignored when I pressed the dumbbells and stood over him. He didn't get the message I could crush him at any time. He's a wise ass weasel. Nor did he get that I played football at Cucamonga Law School. I was the only woman who played college football in the country. I was drafted to play in Canada, but Cucamonga was in my heart.
Who does he think he is?"

"Anyhow, Bonita, you didn't do the job I hired you to do and you're fired.

Benny has moved out of the house and filed Court papers. I tried the magic formula you gave me to get more money from my Roth and it didn't work. I offered him one last time around the maypole and that didn't work either. He checked Cucamonga Law School and found its campus is on Devil's Island."

December

The Honorable **J. Pinkerton Snoopington** reviews the complaint and deliberates: "who is this gate crasher Benny Benefactor and who does he think he is **"Mahatma Kane Jeeves?"** I will dismiss this complaint because of insufficient content."

Bella visits the office of attorney **Mary Hartman Mary Hartman.**

Counselor **Mary Hartman** is middle-aged, five foot seven and 129 pounds. She wears clothing close to her body to accent her musculature honed with devotion. Mary Hartman has prominent cheekbones that support dark, piercing eyes that gives one the impression they are being placed under a microscope. Her hair is straight black and executioner short. Mary Hartman's square jaw exudes foundational stability and power. She sports a Bottega Veneta Single-breasted mohair and wool-blend blazer coordinating with tapered crepe trousers. Her shirt is á Brooks Brothers and Madelyn 55mm Leather Mules with Square G (the 2 inch square heel provides stability in the Courtroom) as footwear. Designer pink bikini panties by Walmart. Bonnet by Kilwinning Archers of Scotland.

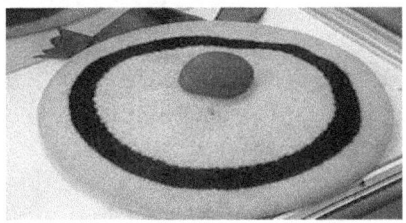

Bella: "I want to keep all of my Roth account and get half from the sale of the house."

Mary Hartman: "maybe, it depends on the numbers and what your husband wants to give you. I need $5,000 as a retainer fee to represent you. Does he drink?"

Bella: he didn't get that nose from playing ping pong. During our honeymoon, when he got up in the morning, he would tremble and quake for hours. It was the only exercise he got. Wait, it got worse. One day he accused me of stealing the cork for his lunch."

Chapter Thirty

Ordinance

Benny receives a letter from counselor Mary Hartman.

My complaint asserted that our house was purchased by separate funds. Mary Hartman claims that if this is true, it doesn't matter since this money became marital property. Hmm, the law states that there is a presumption this is marital property unless I can show separate money was used to buy the house and I did not intend to gift it to Bella. Let's see, the cash used to buy the house came from the sale of my house that I owned before we married. And I have the statements that can trace this to prove this flow of funds. Now this is the sticky part. The law says I have to prove I did not intend to give Bella ownership of the house. Okay, we bought the house in November and in the previous August and May we were close to divorcing. This is the truth, and I will testify in Court that as a result of our unstable marriage, I did not intend to give ownership to Bella.

Mary Hartman says she wants to negotiate this out of Court. I see. She wants to work out a deal that is favorable to Bella. That is what she is getting paid to do. She will use arguments to deny me what I may be able to achieve in Court. Mary Hartman thinks I have the intelligence of a can opener. Bella earned an associate degree in pottery and told me she was going to use this training to start a business. This degree cost about $25,000. The law says I may be able to recover part or all of this. Mary Hartman claims no this is a marital expense and you get nothing. I believe this is a subject of litigation that needs a Court decision. Mary Hartman states that Bella's retirement account is part separate and part marital property. I know this not to be true because Bella's retirement account was accumulated during the marital period. Mary Hartman asserts, her annuity is separate property, and I believe that is subject to negotiation or a Court determination since it was received during the marital period. My margin investment account I can show was funded by my separate funds is claimed by Mary Hartman to be marital assets. This is dead wrong. Okay. The role of Bella's attorney is to deny me my property rights that I may be able to get in Court. She says we do not have to go to Court, give me all the money. This is a repeat of Bella's desires before she hired Mary Hartman. Bella said, give me two thirds of the assets and half of the proceeds from the sale of our house and we can be done. I am too old to work, despite being younger than you, you can go back to work.

An elderly man says to his wife: "the doctor told me the formula to reach a hundred is healthy nutrition, exercise, and sex every day." She says Hymie: "you're going to die early."

Quiz

I believe Mary Hartman's approach with arguments against Benny's claims of ownership of the house and compensation for Bella's pottery degree are her ethical requirements in representing Bella's interest. Support your answer.

I believe (do not), to avoid litigation, Mary Hartman could have adopted an approach different than arguments. Suggest other avenues and defend your answers.

Chapter Thirty-One

Kumite (The Battle Begins)

Benny Benefactor
12 Pauper Row
Hades, NV 00000

Mary Hartman Mary Hartman, Esquire
666 Grand Army Plaza
Brooklyn, N.Y $$$$$

Dear Counselor Mary Hartman:

Thank you for your email dated December 22. This matter will be managed pro se. Discussion will be contained within the boundaries of the statutes and non-controlling and controlling appellate decisions.

    Plaintiff's decisions are guided by the findings of fact, conclusions of law supported by sound reasoning that are subject to a probability function of success.

Perhaps we can agree on a standard of communication. Your email has stated" Hades law is clear on equitable distribution." This statement is a partial truth since the Court will consider the preponderance of evidence regarding the rebuttal of the marital gift presumption.

    Regarding your assertion the associate degree of the defendant is a marital expense is specious.

    § 33-21. Distribution by court of marital and divisible property. (c) There shall be an equal division by using net value of marital property and net value of divisible property unless the court determines that an equal division is not equitable. If the court determines that an equal division is not equitable, the court shall divide the marital property and divisible property equitably. The court shall consider all of the following factors under this subsection:

    Interactive brokerage margin account owned by plaintiff and funded by separate monies from the sale of the separate property Is separate property.

Defendant's annuity is separate and marital property. It's funding prior to the date of marriage would be separate, and funding after the date of marriage up until the point of separation would be marital. If this reasoning is incorrect, please provide case law to refute it.

Benny Benefactor

Do you believe Benny's response was stimulated by Mary Hartman's approach in the previous chapter? Support your answer.

Do you believe Benny's response was thoughtful research? Backup your answer.

What do you believe Mary Hartman should have observed from the content of Benny's letter? If Mary Hartman had a learning experience, should it alter her behavior regarding Benny? How? Defend your answers:

Chapter Thirty-Two

Cloaking (January)

"Hello Bella, you are leaving to stay three weeks in Mexico, and I would like to use the house during this time."

"OK, but I do not want you to have access to the upstairs unit."

"I don't understand Bella, when you went to New York in November I had use of the entire house."

"Your cats were a bad influence on my cat.

Your cats brought catnip into the house and now my cat has a monkey on it's back.

I found him mainlining in the litter box the other day.

The next day he was found in a shooting gallery.

I received a phone call from the police indicating a neighbor claims he broke in and was found rummaging among the plants.

The officer said catnip was a schedule 1 drug and I was a suspect either as an accessory or as a dealer.

My cat was rejected from the 12-step program because he kept rubbing his nose and jumping on people's laps.

You can use the downstairs unit and you won't have access to upstairs because I want privacy regarding my personal stuff."

"Upstairs is the best part of the house and this is where I want to stay."

"I do not want you here and I will have Mary Hartman contact you."

Dear sir, I represent your wife and she doesn't want you to use the house in her absence with the exception of the lower level. Your behavior has indicated to me that the basement would fit your natural habitat and you would be comfortable there.

"I want to use the whole house when she is away and what law prevents me from doing this?" Benny emails this question with this photo:

Dear sir, you will be violating the Domestic Trespass Statute if you insist on occupying the premises while she is away. I will put you in the big house. Not to worry, the latest stockade report indicated that condoms are available for safe sex.

Benny responds OK you win in an email with this photo:

"When I played in the sandbox the cat kept covering me up."
Rodney Dangerfield

QUIZ

Do you think there was an intended message in the Bozo the clown email?

If yes, describe.

If you believe there was a message, should it be a learning experience for Mary Hartman, and should it influence her behavior?

From the content of Benny's letter? If Mary Hartman had a learning experience, should it alter her behavior regarding Benny? How? Defend your answers.

Chapter Thirty-Three

Retainer Disappearance

Mary Hartman: "Bella, your $5,000 retainer has been used. It appears Benny is a troublesome eunuch and I will need another $5,000. Moreover, if there is litigation and depending on its extent, my representation will cost you between $20,000 and $40,000 as an estimate."

Bella: "I'm not giving you more money. I told you I wanted to keep all of my Roth and get half of the money from the house sale. You charged me $5,000 to read his silly emails and keep him out of my house when I go to Mexico. I'm done with it. I'll represent myself; I can't afford your rates and you have not got me what I wanted."

Benny files second summons and complaint for equitable distribution.

He serves Bella document demands and interrogatories under inspection and discovery.

Bella responds with this email.

Where the hell did you get the figure $20,000 - $25,000.00 for a community college 2-year program? Look at the 2016 tax statement. The tuition for 2015 is $1704 and $3605 for 2016. They are all tax deductible. And do you really expect me to make a career out of pottery at 69 years of age? And what about the training you took for investment, real estate, energy audit and house inspection? They were all failures. And what about all the poker loses you incurred playing while I worked my ass out until retirement? Wait till the judge hears all of these.

I set up a trustee account for both Oubliette and Prettywillie, instead of giving them gifts for Christmas and birthdays. Trustee accounts or properties owned by third parties cannot be divided by divorce. Ten years and I only managed to contribute $3,991.43. It's because you are so selfish and self-centered to care about my family. You never had anything positive to say about them - not even associate with them for my sake. Fuck you!

The S&S Roth account and S&S pension are not marital assets, because I earned them during the period when I didn't know you from ADAM (1988-1994).

When I started at Skadden Arps in 2000 and married, I started my 401K contribution only from 2005 through 2009. It so happened that I merged my S&S 401K with SASMF sometime in 2000 to make it easier for me to follow my 401K. My SASMF contributions from 2005 to 2009 was $71,138.00 and is marital asset divisible by 2. That means that your share of my SASMF is 20.68% or $35,569.00. By 2009, you rolled it to TD Ameritrade without my knowledge. You converted it to a Roth account and rolled it over again to Interactive Brokers. The value of my portfolio is more or less $350,000.00 by now. $350,000.00 x 20.68% = $72,380.00 which is what's due you in the equitable distribution.

If you need to, you can pick up the Prudential statements and analysis that came with it.

As to your 2 Roth accounts and margin account, they are marital property and divisible by two. I want the latest statements on these 3 accounts.

Per our written agreement you owe me $5,128.76. Our debt was $27,742.48 divisible by 2. I paid $19,000.00 with a written agreement that this amount will be reconciled during the equitable distribution. You owe me $5,128.76.

Your claim that you purchase 12 Pauper Run with your money is a lie. All the monies we put in as a couple are marital assets/contributions. This is why I stopped digging for the $79,000.00 which you freely invested and played poker with without the decency to ask me. The purchase of 12 Pauper Run was backed by the sale of our house in Ventnor and margin account which we both own as married couple.

I have all the records and tax returns to prove your activities. So do not bullshit me. You barraged my lawyer with your bullshit emails. As a result, I paid almost $5,000.00 for her to respond to you. I gave them instructions to destroy your emails. You will not accomplish anything if you continue sending them emails with your ridiculous clowns.

You are so pathetic. I thought that maybe the meditation will make you better, but hell no. People say the same things about you - You're only interested to talk to them if you can pick their brains. And you use the little knowledge you get to your advantage. Your social skill is zero. Even **Tillie Delight Hemoglobin**, and everyone else, say that you dominate the conversations and think you know everything and is superior to them. She says you'll never make it in real estate because of your personality. Should I be surprised?

QUIZ

I believe Bella has made solid arguments to support her drive to keep her entire Roth account and get half of the money for the sale of Pauper Run. Give reasons.

I believe or do not, Bella has displayed negative emotions in her response, and they are:

Explain your answer.

If I believe Bella has shown harmful emotions, will this have an effect on her behavior and reasoning ability?

Chapter Thirty-Four

Second Opinion

Benny sends this email to Bella.

Putting a settlement offer in the mail today with supporting documents.

It is suggested you get an opinion from an attorney other than Mary Hartman.

She has a strong financial interest in your engaging her services.

She will not be objective.

Larson E. Whipsnade, is a top family lawyer in Hades. 666-999

I had considered using him as a consultant but found it unnecessary.

He will charge you $550 for a consultation.

Please consider bringing him my offer of settlement for his opinion.

The question is will you be better off in the end with large legal bills that deplete your Roth account.

February 12th, we have a pretrial conference.

If you need additional time to decide what to do before engaging Mary Hartman, I will agree to that in Court.

Sound reasoning suggests before you give $5,000 to Mary Hartman that is **not refundable** you have confidence in her ability to recover the cost of her fees with a profit that makes your effort worthwhile.

Moreover, the money you withdraw from your Roth account that is tax free you may not be able to put back. Tax-free income has greater value in the event Mary Hartman does not **produce a profit**. In this scenario, you are reducing your retirement assets as Mary Hartman increases her's.

QUIZ

I believe, or do not, above suggestion (second opinion) is reasonable. If the above idea has value, and Bella rejects it, the reasons are:

Chapter Thirty-Five

Aha

The Next Day
Benny reviews the Consent Order signed in the mediation process.

Hmm, I am to deliver the green rug to Bella. This is strange. Since we divided the two valuable rugs months ago by verbal agreement, she must be talking about a small green rug I have. The green rug description lacks detail.

Wait a minute, the agreement calls for a 48-hour notice to Bella before I can be present for a house showing. This is odd, the house is listed for sale and most buyers do not give a 48-hour notice. Bella wants to exclude me from house showings and there must be a reason. She must be **hiding** something. What could it be? I think there is a link to January when she would not permit me to use the house when she was away for three weeks in Mexico. She went through the expense of having Mary Hartman threaten me with domestic trespass and paid someone to feed her cat. This cost her between $400 and $500

Why?

Now I get it, I left the house in October and I know Bella was not comfortable living there by herself. I suspect Armani had been in contact with her over the years and she invited him to stay in our house in December. She would stay with him in January in Mexico and expect him to live with her in our house in February, until it was sold.

I have no objection to them living together with the exception by law I am entitled to collect rent. Bella has been aware of this since December and her attorney has not acknowledged it. We are splitting the mortgage cost and I am paying rent for my apartment. It is not fair that Bella lives rent-free.

The puzzle is coming together, Armani was in our house in December and left his personal effects and this is why Bella would not permit me to use it in January.

What is the difference between a G-spot and a golf ball?
A man will look for a golf ball.

Chapter Thirty-Six

Romper Room

8:00 a.m. in the bedroom of Armani and Bella at Pauper Run
On the ceiling is a large mirror.
The room is lit by red candles along the perimeter.
The waterbed is covered with black, thick, silk sheets.
There is a statue of Zeus in one corner-he has had his penis & balls severed.
In another corner a statue of Aphrodite who has a penis & balls.
On the walls are pictures of ancient Greek orgies and on a stand a bust of Bacchus.
On a table were the following items bought by Bella on Amazon: "Caged in Chastity. The complete trilogy. The story of a husband's-imposed chastity to his dominant wife!". Kindle Edition, Sissy Pouch Panties Men's Skirted Mooning Bikini Briefs Girly Underwear, a male chastity belt, a harness with a 6 inch dildo.
Bella had a keen awareness of the magnetic eroticism women felt in Armani. By age 60 he had racked up enough conquest to qualify for the Swingers Hall of Fame. To train for his last triathlon, in his Hump Mobile, he explored each state distributing a legacy of pleased ladies. Bella knew younger nubile women lay in wait for Armani. It was time to dominate the bedroom to cement their relationship.
The couple sleeps in pink bikini underwear.
Armani's briefs are bulging.
A moment before awakening Bella stirs, lying on her derriere Armani begins to shimmy her panties down at a relaxed pace.
As Armani lowers his head with pointed tongue and drool, she screeches, no, no, no, Benny is bringing buyers to see the house.
Bella hoist her panties and springs out of the bed.
She covers up the statues and the bust with cloth.
She hands the male chastity belt, Sissy Pouch Panties and harness to Armani and says "you and these have to disappear." Bella leads him into the garage where there is a trap door to the attic. In a frenzy he scampers up the ladder but fails to close the trap door in its entirety.

Benny and the buyers arrive.

They do their walk through the house with the garage being the last stop.

When they enter the garage, the buyer's wife looks up and she sees a dangling dildo and the Sissy Pouch Panties caught in the trap door. She looks at Bella and says" was it fun?"

Chapter Thirty-Seven

Rug Delivery

Okay, Bella wants the green rug I have but I want to avoid her presence since the last time we met she hurled curses and death wishes at me. We are to meet where the mailboxes are, and I have emailed her I will throw the rug out the window of my car.

Wait a minute, despite that Mary Hartman has threatened me with domestic trespass I will deliver the rug at five in the morning on the porch of our house.

Benny delivers the rug to the porch.

Later that morning.

Bella phones Benny.

"This is not the rug I want; I want the large green rug."

Benny says: "Oh, you're talking about the Hereke rug. You may remember, months ago, we divided the two valuable rugs, you chose the Tree of Life and that left me with the Hereke. The Consent Order did not give a description of the green rug and I believe the one I delivered to you was the one in the Consent Order. This matter had been settled and if Mary Hartman had given a description of the green rug, I would not have agreed to the one that you want."

The next day.

Mary Hartman emailed Benny and demanded he turn over the green rug.

A woman gives birth to a baby and afterward the doctor comes into the room and says, "I have something to tell you about your child ..."
The woman slowly sits up with a worried look on her face and says, "What's wrong with it?"
The doctor says, "There's nothing really wrong with it, it's just a little different! It's a hermaphrodite."
The woman looks confused. "A hermaphrodite, what's that?"
The doctor replies, "It has both features of a male and a female."
The woman looks relieved. "What? You mean it has a penis and a

brain?"

Benny emails Ms. Mary Hartman: "I delivered the rug I thought was in the agreement. You did not describe it in detail and I would not have agreed to give the rug that she wants."
Hartman's response: "you are in violation of the Court Order and I can have the Court put you in the pokey unless you pony up the rug."

What do you call a man who won't go down on you?
You don't.

Benny: "If you do that, I will sue for breach of contract and now I get why you put the 48-hour notice in the Consent Order. The reason was to give well hung Amorous Armani time not to get caught with his pants down and button his fly.

"Life is divided into the horrible and the miserable."- Woody Allen.
I believe Bella nurtured a relationship with Armani over the years, kept him panting until she was ready to push the seat ejection button (James Bond, Goldfinger). This may be alienation of affection as regards Armani and the possibility of adultery for Bella. You file for civil contempt, and, I'll respond in kind."
An elderly man took care of his body. He lifted weights and jogged six miles every day. One morning he looked into the mirror admiring his body and noticed that he was suntanned all over with the exception of his penis. He decided to do something about that. He went to the beach, undressed and buried himself in the sand except for his penis which he left sticking out of the sand.

Later, two senior ladies came strolling along the beach, one using a cane to help her get along. Upon seeing the thing sticking out of the sand the lady with the cane began to move the penis around with her cane.

Remarking to the other lady, she said, "There is no justice in the world. "The other lady asked, "What do you mean?"

The first lady replied, "Look at that. When I was 20, I was curious about it. When I was 30, I enjoyed it.

When I was 40, I asked for it. When I was 50, I paid for it. When I was 60, I prayed for it. When I was 70, I forgot about it.

" Now that I'm 80, the damned things are growing wild, and I'm too old to squat."

Chapter Thirty-Eight

Alienation of Affection

OK, Mary Hartman is ornery in going after a $500 rug. I will have to see what I can do about it.

Benny reviews the Consent Order.

This agreement is silent on who gets use and occupancy of our home. The law has said that if one spouse has exclusive occupancy of the marital home, the other spouse is entitled to rent. I had brought this motion before we signed the Consent Order and it was not addressed by the Court. Photos on Facebook show Armani has been living with Bella from February to at least the end of May. My concern is not her banging Armani, it is with collecting rent. However, since he is well hung, I will consider charging him with alienation of affection. Moreover, Mary Hartman knew I desired to collect rent and with intent excluded it from the Consent Order. This is a misrepresentation that I will argue to have the Consent Order modified enabling me to collect rent. These aggressions taken by me are common in litigation. One party initiates a hostile action and the other party respond in kind.

Often from a legal or financial standpoint there is little change and the legal bills escalate until exhaustion.

Dear Ms. Mary Hartman:

1) I know for a fact well before the date of separation a neighbor had informed me a close friend of his had wanted to get into Bella's pants. This person is referred to as Armani and I met him at a party on Sky-high Mountain.

> *"My wife only has sex with me for a purpose. Last night she used me to time an egg."* Rodney Dangerfield

2) I believe, since Bella wanted to give Armani extra time to vamoose (the 48 hour notice in the Consent Order) while he frolicked in the merriment of Bella's bed and board. This can be verified in inspection and discovery.

3) If two above is true, it is unfair, since Bella is living in a luxury house, rent free, on Sky-high Mountain and they are randy on a free roll.

4) If Armani is getting it on with Bella, I will file a complaint against him if it can be shown that he was attracting Bella with his prodigious naughty bits.

5) It is suggested you do not file the Consent Decree and we change it so I get rental income during Bella's romp. I don't believe in free fucks unless they are mine.

> *"I spit on education. When a man puts his hand up a women's dress, he is not looking for a library card."*   Joan Rivers

AA may have made several visits to our home after he expressed to his friend that Bella elevated more than the spirit in him. I remember Armani told me he had many divorces and mucho women who all enjoyed multiple orgasms.

> *"Women find me Tasty."* Mick Jagger

The evidence will be collected until sufficient data is available to submit to the District Attorney for criminal prosecution. Since Armani is making it with Bella, he is responsible for my massive suffering. I feel the sting of leather on my back as I stumble along the road to Calvary. I winch as I see the cross planted in the earth. Dark clouds congregate and thunder rumbles. Straps across my wrists and ankles bind. I am skewered with spikes in my hands and feet as I am mounted on the cross.

Armani Is the Romeo. Memory serves that he was elderly, and, maybe not capable of cuming.

As a sexual partner, he is crotchety, and, may be limited to cunnilingus.

"Kinky is using a feather. Perverted is using the whole chicken." ~ Anon

If Bella can reach an orgasm this way, that is wonderful.

However, this Is a stone in my shoe.

Please ask Bella to enjoy Rambo, after she pays rent.

I do not believe orgasms are free unless they are mine.

If this can be done, I will not respond.

Bella should enjoy as many orgasms as she likes, they promote health.

I do object to Armani spreading his seed on my dime.

Thank you

QUIZ

What do you think Benny desired to achieve with above emails?

I believe (do not) Benny was suffering from the loss of Bella.

Why?

Chapter Thirty-Nine

A Blocked Sewer Explodes

The second day after the agreement was reached.

Benny's experiences.

In the morning I did yoga, Pilates and cardiovascular training. My body sensations have an exceptional positivity. About 11 a.m. I am surprised by feelings of anxiety. There is a creeping unsettling vibration in my shoulders. I am aware this is a chemical reaction that has negative consequences. After Identifying this feeling as anxiety, I am shocked. My deep and long-term meditation practice had enabled me to be free of anxiety regardless of stressful situations.

Horrible, conflicts in feelings are flooding my consciousness. They are irrational and make me feel terrible. They appear to have a life of their own and are not controllable. If I deny them, they resurface with greater force. My mind trembles in horror. My meditation practice has given me great focus and clarity of mind. This skill has been weakened by an anxiety attack. Negative sensations are flooding my existence and they have free will to do as they please. They are unstoppable and painful. Why?

There is a tension of panic. If I try to dismiss these feelings, they gathered speed. I am a train that has run away, speeding, awful feelings, dread. The master of the mind has now become the obedient servant. As the day progresses the dark sentiment accompanies each thought. There are brief gaps of clarity without apprehension. This is a welcomed oasis; however, the demons resurface with continuing torture. When will it stop. I do not know. There is no place to hide. If these feelings continue, I will fall into depression.

Recovery/Resilience

That evening I meditated for one hour. This reduced anxiety and quieted the mind. Amazing, simple practice of sitting in a half lotus position with a straight back for one hour has provided peace and comfort. I had thought the torture was unbridled and not being subject to taming.

After breaking the sit, I observed a decrease in stress. No, it did not disappear. However, the torture has a lower vibration. My mind said I will punish you less but not go away. Despite the reduction in misery there was a large distance from my customary emotional state. The speed of my thoughts had decreased in frequency. If the sickness continued, I faced a life of sadness. Beset with unwelcomed never-ending negative energy bereft of regulation.

Lying in bed, trying to relax the body and the mind can't be done. The pool of poison begins to bubble up. All impressions get stored in the unconscious. They sleep until disturbed either by life events or active inducement (meditation). Meditation enables one to pay close attention to body sensations. These sensitivities are the language of the subconscious. Your body reports the landscape of your interior life.

The next day, awaken at 5 AM. Surprised by energy level considering restless sleep because of the drip, drip of creepy body sensations. Began writing journal of these events. Notice the act of writing reduces the suffering. As the morning wears on the irritating aspects of PTSD subside. I speculate, they will not go away at once, but I am pleased they are on the wane. Going forward I get an inside view of how my neurology works. It is free of judgment in response to the immediate environment. My marriage was dysfunctional and terminating it was a healthy decision. Intellectually I feel great to have ended a relationship that was harmful to each of us. Separation is a form of death as in loss. Being human I have a strong desire to be connected with another person. Until my neurology learns new responses with the associated body sensations, the past will be present. Social contact being involved in an activity, exercise and meditation are the medications for the current situation. Positive behaviors and time will provide healing.

No, it has not ended. Bella and I have a dispute over a rug. I explained to her that each of us had a choice of which rug to choose which we each did. Now she claims both rugs belong to her. This is not true. I am feeling worn by our continuous conflict and remark you will have to sue me for it.

Two days later I received a Show Cause Order by Mary Hartman asserting contempt of the Consent Order. I have to appear in Court before the judge with an explanation. Mary Hartman has taken an extreme measure rather than attempt to solve the problem in a non-aggressive manner, Mary Hartman threatens fines, imprisonment, and attorney fees. Our Consent Order distributed about $850,000 in assets, Mary Hartman is using maximum force regarding a $500 rug. Throughout our litigation this is a repeating pattern, Mary Hartman takes aggressive action and I respond with equal or greater aggression. Each party continues without abatement. **The result is a spiral of hostility with mounting legal bills.**

The ball is in my court and I respond with four motions attempting to have the Consent Order voided. I offer a simple solution to Mary Hartman and it is rejected with a comment "there is nothing to negotiate, the Consent Order is done, and it is time for you to move on." Next stop an appearance before the judge regarding Contempt of the Court.

"Everybody talks about multiple orgasms. Multiple orgasm — I'm lucky if both sides of my toaster pop." Joan Rivers.

Chapter Forty

Show Cause Order

    Benny opens his mail and finds an order to appear in Court to explain why he has not given the rug to Bella.

    Okay I got it; the first cannon has fired. This Show Cause Order states that there is probable cause that I have violated the Consent Order. I must find out what probable cause means. It says here Judge **J. Pinkerton Snoopington** believes that I may be guilty, and the Court is giving me a chance to explain myself. This is *curious*, it appears I start out being accused by Mary Hartman as to not complying with the Consent Order. Strange, the Court believes I am guilty, but I am given a chance to exonerate myself. I start out on the defensive.

    It is time to put on the war paint.

"I'm short enough and ugly enough to succeed on my own." —Woody Allen, Annie Hall: Screenplay

I believe (do not) Mary Hartman's response to Benny's disagreement regarding a $500 rug by applying the Show Cause Order was an effective action on behalf of Bella. Why?

I believe (do not) Hartman should have estimated the value of the rug in relation to expected *legal costs*. Why?

    Okay, it appears Mary Hartman is preparing for combat. We have an honest dispute regarding a rug that has an approximate market value of $500. I know I did not intend to give the Hereke rug to Bella. Mary Hartman is responsible for this confusion as a result of her failure to describe the rug in the Consent Order.

Chapter Forty-One

The War Room

Okay, I got it, in three weeks I go to a hearing where the judge believes I am in contempt of the Court, because I have not turned over the green rug. This is the most aggressive action that could be taken by Mary Hartman since the Court can put me in the pokey.

"I tell ya, my wife was never nice. On our first date, I asked her if I could give her a goodnight kiss on the cheek – she bent over!" Rodney Dangerfield

We are dealing with a $500 rug over a simple dispute. This could have been done in Small Claims Court or mediation or arbitration.

I believe I have an equal right to be aggressive in the face of aggression.

Benny files the following motions:

Request for rental reimbursement since Bella is living rent-free in their home

Request for his legal cost if the Court does not find him in contempt

Request to set aside Consent Order and award rental reimbursement because the Order did not deal with use and occupancy of the premises

Modify the Consent Order because a 48-hour notice was required before Benny could be present for a real estate showing

Request Bella cooperate with the sale of the property by returning phone calls to Benny

Request the Court to order Bella to cease and desist from slandering Benny

Request the Court strikes the Defendants Motion

Request the right to give testimony in Court

Request the right to rent the marital residence

Improper pleading, request the Court to bring the issue of the ownership of the green rug to Small Claims Court

Request the Court dismiss the Show Cause Order

Request the Court grant separate ownership of the marital property

Request the Court clarify if the contempt is civil, criminal or both
Request a trial by the Court
Response to Mary Hartman seeking legal fees
Request of oral deposition of Bella
Request for interrogatories to be completed by Bella
Brief

Sex is one of the nine reasons for reincarnation... the other eight are unimportant.

Henry Miller

Mary Hartman phones Bella.
"The $2,500 you gave me to pursue Benny for the green rug is gone. It has turned out the slug is a hard nut to crack. I thought he would whimper and slink away when Snoopington threatened him with jail time. He has the biggest pair of cojones I have seen in the Court. He thinks they are wrecking balls and he is more well hung than Armani."

Bella: "Look Mary Hartman, you told me you and Snoopington would be able to handle Benny and get him to cough up the rug and the cost would be $2,500. I have given you about $25,000 and you have produced nothing but bills. I won't give you a penny more and I want the rug.

What is your opinion regarding Bella's refusal to pay Mary Hartman more money?

Are you able to copy Bella's behavior?

Chapter Forty-Two

Contempt of Court

Three weeks later in the District Court.
Sir, do you understand you are in deep doo-doo, stated Judge J. Pinkerton Snoopington? He wore an Obey Clothing Smokestack Trucker Hat. In the front panel of the hat was a 4-inch square with a small yellow trim, a red background that has superimposed a tractor symbol that is white and within the symbol, in red capital letters, the word obey.

I can send you up the river and whack you with a fine. I received my monthly report of prison conditions in the state and it is my duty to provide you this information.

Our prisons are under a Federal District Court Order to reduce overcrowding, lice infestation, botulism and rape. Further, the solitary confinement cells are to have painted windows with curtains added and Perry Como music piped in. In the last prison riot the jailbirds demanded 2-ply bathroom tissue and personal lubricant in the interest of hygiene and fun. They have been awarded.

Snoopington bellowed you have the right to an attorney.

Benny trembled and noted a sprinkle of urine trickling down his leg. He was seated and his body began to rock in the chair. The words tumbled out of his mouth.

"Oh, oh, oh, K."

That afternoon, at the office of **Og Oggilby**.

Og tapped his black bowler hat as he leaned towards Benny, before we talk do you agree to pay me $500 per hour for an hour or less consultation?

Yes.

The Court has ordered a hearing if I don't turn over a rug that is in dispute. The rug is worth about $500.

"Let me see the Order."

Og attaches a monocle and reads the Order.

"My son you are in a heap of trouble. Snoopington believes you have misbehaved, and you are in danger of going to the stockade. Snoopington's lineage can be traced back to Judge Roy Bean. Snoopington is the Justice of the Peace of Hades. Do you know what can happen to you in the big house? Did Snoopington read you the monthly prison report?"

"Yes, sir."

"You can hire me to represent you, but I can't promise you will be able to keep the rug nor that I can keep you out of the slammer. If Snoopington decides to box your ears, I may be able to plea bargain for you and that will depend on his mood.

Son are you a God-fearing man?"

"Yes sir.""

"Let us kneel together and pray for your redemption."

"I don't think my parents liked me. They put a live teddy bear in my crib."   Woody Allen

To provide the proper service to you I need a $5,000 retainer and I bill at $500 an hour plus other expense. The $5,000 is not refundable since it considered a subway, it goes down south at once.

Benny writes out a check for $500 for the consultation that lasted 10 minutes.

Thank you, sir, I'll let you know if I want to engage your service.

"I have no sex appeal; if my husband didn't toss and turn, we'd never would have had the kid." Joan Rivers

Chapter Forty-Three

The Show Cause Hearing for Contempt.

Hartman: "Your honor, Benny entered into a Consent Order signed by this Court to deliver the green rug to my client.

The day before the green rug was to be delivered Benny at 5 a.m. delivered a small green rug on the porch of the residence. This rug had been used as a doormat."

Benny (in thought) "no I do not recall this rug being used as a doormat and I thought this was the rug described in the Consent Order."

Hartman:" The next day he sent an email to me about his concern over an alleged romantic rival."

"My wife wants sex in the back of the car, and she wants me to drive."
Rodney Dangerfield

Benny (in thought) "No I did not consider Armani a rival, I knew he wanted to boff Bella years ago and I was grateful Bella kept him in heavy breath. He is my hero.

"Take my wife, please." Henny Youngman

The recent Facebook photos of Armani and Bella as a happy couple in the city where my home used to be is not an allegation, it is a fact."

Your honor, exclaimed Mary Hartman, "the email also remarked about the deep wounds Benny felt as a result of Armani's pandering."

Benny (in thought) "Mary Hartman does not see the humor in this email, I was pleased Armani was on the scene. Did Hartman believe I felt I was being crucified?"

"Your honor another email from Mr. Benny, titled failed orgasm, suggested he was withholding the rug because Armani was is in the saddle depriving him of the pleasures of Bella. And your honor in a motion he tried to have the Consent Order nullified because of the hanky panky of Senator Armani.

Your honor, this gentleman is of advanced age, but my client has assured me he is capable of cutting the mustard. I had his total testosterone level tested and it came in at 811 and that exceeds the typical male of age 25. Bella has told me he is well hung with hydraulic power (Bella Giggled when she heard this in Court). Moreover, he has maintained cardiovascular fitness enabling him to forgo Viagra. I will stipulate his penis isn't what it used to be. However, it does complete the mission. Benny has libeled Armani because the diddling privileges have been transferred from him to Senator Armani.

As an officer of the Court, I swear these statements to be true."

Benny (in thought) "I can't believe it, I felt Armani was doing me a favor by taking Bella off my hands My objection was they were both living there rent-free, and I was entitled to collect rent, nothing more."

Benny examines Bella under oath in Court.

"Do you recall you and Benny met in September to divide the contents of your house?

"Yes," answered Bella.

"Do you recall Benny indicated there were two rugs of equal value to be divided, one was the Tree of Life and the other was the Hereke, and you could choose which one you wanted?"

"Yes," Bella responded.

"Which one did you choose?"

"The Tree of Life, "said Bella.

"Thank you, we are done."

Benny takes the stand and gives this testimony.

"The Consent Order described the green rug without detail. I believed this was the rug that I delivered because there was no reason for me to believe that our original agreement in dividing the two rugs of equal value had changed. If Mary Hartman had made it clear what green rug, they were talking about there would never have been an agreement and possibly a Consent Order."

Three weeks later-the court rules.

The Court has concluded that the couple referred to the Hereke rug as the green rug and this is the green rug reference in the Consent Order.

Benny muses ("I have never referred to it as the green rug)."

The Court declares that Benny's refusal to deliver the large green Turkish Hereke rug is a willful violation of the Consent Order. For the purposes of this Order, the subject carpet is the large green Turkish Hereke carpet.

Benny's thoughts ("Snoopington has modified the Consent Order to describe the green rug to support the ruling)".

The Court declares that the actions of Benny are without just cause and are intentional and malicious.

Benny's thoughts "I believed the ownership of the two rugs was settled months before and Snoopington says this is not a reasonable cause to resist turning over the rug.

Moreover, Snoopington says my behavior was malicious because I was upset about Senator Armani cavorting with Bella. This is the opposite of the truth. The Senator has put an end to my misery and suffering."

A woman accompanied her husband to the doctor's office.
After his checkup, the doctor called the wife into his office alone. He said,
"Your husband is suffering from a very severe stress disorder. If you don't follow my instructions carefully, your husband will surely die.
"Each morning fix him a healthy breakfast. Be pleasant at all times. For lunch make him a nutritious meal. For dinner prepare an extra nice meal for him.
"Don't give him chores. Keep your problems to yourself. Do not nag him."
"Do this for the next year, and your husband will regain his health."
The husband asked his wife, "What did the doctor say?"
"He said you're going to die."

Mary Hartman Mary Hartman to Snoopington.

Your honor, here is a motion for $5,160 in <u>legal cost</u> I would like you to tax Benny for.

Benny responds, "your honor, my papers prove the current market value of this rug is about $500. Bella could have brought this action in Small Claims Court or by mediation or arbitration and by State Law she had a duty to do this to mitigate damages. The intent of the law was to reduce expensive litigation and fairness does not justify charging me $5,160 to recover a $500 rug."

"I am ruling to pass the motion and you are ordered to pay. Your behavior has been pernicious, and this is the cost. Further, this Court holds your testimony was an act of perjury. By not surrendering the rug you were punishing your coveted, innocent wife. Your emails proved you believed you were being crucified. You were disconcerted Senator Armani had acquired your porking privileges.

Hartman: "your honor, this is a motion to recover <u>legal costs</u> for frivolous motions Benny entered after the Consent Order has been finalized. He has exhibited disrespect for the law by ignoring the clear message of this Court that his obedience was required. The amount is $4,313."

Snoopington: "I agree counselor, I will grant your motion and order him to pay. His motions are without basis in law, logic, or extension of law. Except for his request for rental income and for the Court to decide the ownership of the marital residence his motions are not warranted.

"May I address the Court your honor" inquired Benny?"

Snoopington nods.

"The Consent Order settled $850,000 in assets.

Mary Hartman threatens me with the most extreme action of incarceration with the Show Cause Order.

Each motion I did was based on fact or law and many were responses to Bella's behavior, one would be where I submitted proof, she was slandering me to neighbors. I claim the right to respond to Mary Hartman's aggression with thoughtful. counterpoints."

"Nonetheless, Snoopington brayed I am ordering you to pay the money, turn over the rug or Sheriff John Hoxley will put you in handcuffs and deliver you to a penal colony. You signed the Consent Order on April 3rd and as Mary Hartman has pointed out this matter was closed. Because of your emotional wounds you withheld the carpet for revenge. Mary Hartman had the sole right to recover the carpet and you have no right to resist this. Mary Hartman and I have advised you to seek professional Counsel and you spurned Og Oggilby.

He pounded his gavel causing tremors in the room.

"My luck is getting worse and worse. Last night, for instance, I was mugged by a Quaker." — *Woody Allen*

Chapter Forty-Four

A Model to Manage Your Financial Future

What follows is a program to minimize the cost of a contested divorce.

Regardless of the emotional climate, meaning one or both spouses may be at war.

Do not hire Mary Hartman or Bonita Broadbottom.

Lawyers do not accept Mazuma Play Money.

Bring in an accountant.

The goal is to put the assets on the table with complete transparency.

The parties manage the situation as a financial transaction without emotion.

The accountant will issue these findings.

Assets will be separated into personal property, real estate and liquid Investments (stock brokerage accounts, annuities, life insurance, mortgages held or other assets that provide a stream of income or value). Business assets are to be detached from personal assets and enumerated as above.

Assets that are owned prior to the marriage and remain separate during the marital period are excluded from above findings.

Real estate ownership will be determined by how it is deeded.

Marital assets are those that are accumulated during the matrimonial period. This wealth is independent of who contributed it.

The couple can consider a mediator to reach an agreement on the division of the assets if there is resentment between the couple.

Good Luck, Namaste

Index

Accountant	43
Anger	2,27,29,30,38,39,48,53,66
Attorney Bill	22
Collaborative Law Model	28
Detachment	26,27,29
Do Not	31,33,34,35,37,41,45,49,62,64,67,111
Do Not Sign	54,55
Fear	2,27,29,38,62
Goals	26,27,39,41,42,45,49,54,58,111
Intuition	31,33,49
Legal Cost	26,35,58,66,101
Revenge	41,49
Stress Management	36
Value	19,29,34,39,40,45,46,47,49,50,55,101

Acknowledgement

Profound gratitude to the friends who have contributed to enrich this work: Jim Cox, Art Acacossa, Linda Greenup and Frank Benedetto.

Notes

www.ingramcontent.com/pod-product-compliance
Lightning Source LLC
Chambersburg PA
CBHW070651220526
45466CB00001B/390